FIRE

of

LOVE

FIRE

of

LOVE

Praying with Thérèse of Lisieux

By
James McCaffrey, OCD

BOOKS & MEDIA
Boston

Contents

Preface   ix

1   **Carmelite Origins**   1

Elijah: Father of the Carmelites   2

The First Carmelites   4

Mary: Patron, Mother, and Sister   6

Christ-Centered: The Carmelite Rule   8

Teresa of Avila and John of the Cross   9

Thérèse: Sister in the Faith   9

Reflections   11

2   **A Saint for Our Season**   15

Beginnings   15

Life at Carmel   17

Lessons from Thérèse's Life   21

Reflections   27

3   **Jesus: My Only Love!**   31

Weakness Is the Key   32

A Thirst for Love   35

Strength Through Weakness,
Love from Pain   38

Reflections   44

4   **Like Little Children**   47

The Call to Conversion   48

A Time for Love   50

The Little Way   52

With Empty Hands   55

The Cost of Surrender   56

Reflections   59

5   The Burning Heart   61

God's Enduring Love   61

The New Heart   63

Reflections   73

6   Prayer   77

A Surge of the Heart   77

A Thinking Heart   80

An Expanding Heart   83

Open to the Spirit   86

Reflections   91

7   Repentance   95

Homecoming   96

A Fragile Church   99

The Pharisee Within   103

A Fresh Start   105

Reflections   108

Select Bibliography   112

Preface

ON OCTOBER 19, 1997 (Mission Sunday in the centenary of her death), Pope John Paul II officially proclaimed St. Thérèse of Lisieux a Doctor of the Church in Rome. How ironic it is that since Thérèse's deepest desire was to remain "hidden, unknown and forgotten," she now finds herself among those whom she called "holy doctors who illumine the Church with the clarity of their teaching"—and only twenty-four years of age! God never ceases to baffle the wise.

But Thérèse is not a doctor in the traditional sense: someone outstanding in holiness, whose teaching has universal appeal. She is a doctor with a difference; she breaks the mold. Her teaching is not a systematic or dogmatic synthesis. It is contained within a story—her life story—like the teaching of Jesus in the Gospels. Her lessons are grace-laden reflections on her experiences as a woman. She speaks with a woman's heart. She offers a refreshing change from a traditional, rational approach to the Gospels; she is a challenge to a Church so long out of touch with its own feminine roots. She is a sure guide to the maternal heart of God.

Thérèse is also young—not just in age, but in mind and spirit, too. Significantly, her future doctorate was first announced at an international gathering of young people in Paris. She speaks to the young with a vision that is fresh, youthful, and childlike. She is a reassuring voice to those for whom wisdom is always young. "From the youth of St. Thérèse," wrote John Paul II, "spring forth her enthusiasm for the Lord, the intensity of her love, and her realistic daring. The charm of her holiness is confirmation that God grants in abundance, even to the young, the treasures of wisdom."

Despite her great achievement, however, her life is a celebration of littleness. But this is often misunderstood. She says something deep and meaningful for most of us who live our lives in the ordinary, sometimes tedious grind of humdrum duties. For her, this is where greatness lies. She had already proclaimed the message of Vatican II that holiness is for everyone. She has been rightly called "the saint of the Council," its prophet and forerunner.

Her central message of surrendering in weakness to God's merciful love is a message of hope for a Church struggling in a postmodern age with its own weaknesses, scandals, and sinfulness. She lays bare the fragile human heart of priest and lay Christian alike. God enters through our wounds, she tells us. Her life is an invitation to rediscover the Gospel lesson of the "anawim," the "little ones," beloved of God, who inherit the kingdom, and to rediscover that the Church is not a lifeless pyramid of sterile and meaningless institutions, but a "heart burning with love."

Thérèse is a saint with the common touch. Dorothy Day rightly said of her: "On the frail battleground of her flesh were fought out the wars of today." She is one with all of us, even atheists, who are anguished by the silence of God—desolate, lonely, abandoned. She, too, struggled with her own emptiness. She witnesses to everyone with her faith that was refined and tested in "the night of nothingness." She reaches out to all who sincerely seek the truth.

In our culture of death with abortion, euthanasia, and assisted suicide, Thérèse reaffirms that life is sacred and love is primary. Nothing became her in her own life like the leaving of it. But she did not regard it as dying; rather, she was "entering into life." For her, every kind of pain—rejection, poverty, failure, discrimination, AIDS—even death itself, could be transformed into an experience of love not just endured stoically.

Her kind of witness, unseen by the world at large, is at the core of the new evangelization, the missionary outreach of the Church today. It is a witness of struggle and growth in Christian living, a reaching out "with empty hands" in prayer, imploring mercy for herself and others, and a death accepted with love.

Thérèse discovers everything in the gentle arms of her Lover. He is weak like herself, and passionately in need of love, like herself. He is "Jesus, my only friend...Jesus, my only love."

1

Carmelite Origins

MOST PEOPLE TODAY have heard of St. Thérèse of Lisieux, but perhaps not everyone knows that she was a Carmelite or even what it means to be a Carmelite. To begin our history of Thérèse, we must first look to the origins of the Carmelite movement, founded on the remote and inaccessible heights of Mount Carmel, a prominent landmark in the north of the Holy Land.

Thérèse used the word "Carmel" repeatedly in her writings to describe her religious and spiritual home. "Carmel" is a biblical term derived from the Hebrew word "karem," meaning "vineyard" or "garden" (with the additional suffix "l" for the Divine name "el," it can also mean "the garden or the vineyard of the Lord"). More accurately, however, it describes a kind of woodland adorned with a rich variety of shrubs, wild flowers, and small trees, much like Mount Carmel is today. "Carmel" is also a biblical symbol for beauty and fruitfulness, used, for example, by the spouse in the Song of Songs in order to praise the beauty of his beloved (7:5).

Elijah: Father of the Carmelites

In St. Peter's Basilica, Rome, stands an imposing sculpture of the prophet Elijah holding a flaming sword and pointing his finger heavenward. Underneath the figure is a plaque which explains that "the entire Carmelite Order erected [it] to its Founder." This statue, unveiled in 1727 after the official approval of Pope Benedict XIII, shows the huge importance that the Carmelite Order gives to its founder. Its beginnings were certainly momentous.

Mount Carmel has been regarded as a place of worship from time immemorial. It was sacred to the pagan god Zeus, and there, on its heights, a gigantic contest was fought by a fiery prophet of Israel—Elijah—against the false prophets of another pagan god, Baal, in a struggle for the hearts of God's people. This contest remains an inspiration to the Order we now know as Carmelite, and leaves an indelible stamp on Carmelite spirituality—that of the importance of persevering in prayer.

The story of the contest between Elijah and Baal is told in First Kings 18 with dramatic effect. In Canaanite mythology, Baal was the god of fertility who gave rain and fruitfulness to the earth. The hearts of the Israelites had strayed to this idol from the pure worship of the one true God. Elijah had to call the Israelites to renewal and conversion and to return to the God of the covenant.

The people were wavering, hesitating, dithering. Their hearts were divided. Elijah challenged them: "How long will you hobble first on one leg, then on another? If Yahweh is God, follow him; if Baal, follow him" (v. 21). The prophets of Baal stormed heaven with frantic gestures, even the shedding of blood, and with wild cries of delirium. But no one answered them; no one heeded their calls. The god of the elements was silent. "Perhaps he is asleep, or on a journey," Elijah mocked. The wild orgy continued until the evening, but in vain. Then Elijah prayed with calm and quiet assurance: "Yahweh, God of Abraham, Isaac, and Israel, let them know today that you are God...and are winning back their hearts" (v. 37). God answered with fire. "Yahweh is God!" the people cried, "Yahweh is God!" (v. 39). The contest ended; there could be no compromise. Yahweh alone is God!

Thus Elijah emerged as a great model of prayer, particularly in the story of the rains coming to end a prolonged drought (1 Kings 18:41–46). Elijah asked his servant to go up and look toward the sea. The servant went and looked, and said, "There is nothing." Heaven was silent. But Elijah called for determination and perseverance in the emptiness. "Go up seven times," he urged. On the seventh time, "Behold, a little cloud like a man's hand is rising out of the sea." The heavens "grew black with clouds and wind, and there was a great rain."

The trials of Elijah did not end with victory on Mount Carmel. He faced a relentless pursuit by Queen Jezebel, and a period of soul-searching in the wilderness where he begged God to take his life, since he was "no better than my fathers." In these depths of failure, loneliness, and despair, however, he miraculously received sustenance to help him on his journey, actually enabling him to travel for forty days and nights to Mount Horeb, the mountain of God. There, the revelation of God to Elijah was not in the dazzling splendor of Sinai, nor in the devouring fire from heaven of Mount Carmel. Rather, it was in silence. The Lord was not in the wind, nor in the earthquake, nor in the fire, but in the still, small voice, like the whisper of a gentle breeze (1 Kings 19:11–13). The prophet who had called others to "conversion" had to experience it for himself. The deepening of Elijah's relationship with God through this radical conversion took on for him the pattern of an "exodus," recalling the desert experience of the people of God.

Elijah knew that he must now retrace his steps at God's command and return to his prophetic task of proclaiming God's word, and continue his ministry renewed and transformed. "Then the prophet Elijah arose like a fire, and his word burned like a torch" (Sirach 48:1). The gift of his spirit fell to his successor, Elisha, and his disciples after him.

The First Carmelites

Elijah may have appeared suddenly on the stage of salvation history and then disappeared in a chariot of fire (2 Kings 2:11), but his spirit survived in the group of people who lived like hermits in the caves on the slopes of Mount Carmel toward the end of the twelfth century. These people were drawn to the sacred mountain by the feats of Elijah and Elisha; they were "palmers" or Western pilgrims to the Holy Land. Jacques de Vitry, Bishop of Acre (1216–1228), described them as "devout pilgrims who had settled on Mount Carmel by the spring of Elijah [who] were leading a life of solitude in small cells, where—like bees in a hive—they gathered the sweetest honey of divine contemplation, imitating the example of the holy and solitary prophet Elijah."

Albert, Patriarch of Jerusalem, gave a Rule to this group of hermits in response to their own wishes, "in keeping with your avowed purpose," between 1206 and 1214. This Rule was designed to codify in a flexible way the original inspiration that had already begun to define itself among the hermits themselves, and to mature gradually and progressively through lived experience. "Pondering the Lord's law day and night and watching in prayer" (the lectio divina) was their principal work. Prayer and contemplation were the priority, the soul of the Rule, which continues to this day. Everything in the Carmelite Rule is designed to foster and preserve, deepen and express this essential core of prayer and contemplation—silence, solitude, love for one another, self-denial, even manual work.

Pope Honorius III approved Albert's Primitive Rule in 1226, but circumstances soon began to change. In 1238, the Carmelites on Mount Carmel, under threat of persecution, gradually began to drift back to their own countries of origin. They finally disappeared from Mount Carmel after the destruction of Acre in 1291, and would not return there for another three centuries. The Rule was corrected, amended, and then approved by Pope Innocent IV in 1247, but the ancient eremitical or solitary lifestyle of old had been enriched with a new community dimension. The ruins of the first Carmelite oratory and refectory bear witness to this change. In the new community, decisions would be made collectively under the authority of a superior or prior, chosen by common consent, to be the father of the community. Meals were taken together as the community listened to the reading of the Scriptures. The choral recitation of the Divine Office took place in a chapel newly erected for that purpose, as did the daily celebration of the Eucharist. The Carmelite fellowship was inspired by the breaking of the bread, and was united in mind and heart by the bond of love.

Mary: Patron, Mother, and Sister

The hermits chose Mary as the patron of their first chapel. To be a Carmelite was to be consecrated to the "Blessed Mary of Mount Carmel" by religious profession and to be clothed in her scapular—the special sign of Carmelite devotion to Mary. It was destined to become, in the words of Pope Paul VI, "a devotion of the whole Church" and is accepted and approved by the Church today as a sign of Mary's motherly care and protection for all the people of God who choose to wear it.

Mary was first honored by Carmelites as Domina, that is, Lady or Mistress. This was a title conditioned by a feudal world-view prevalent at the time of the Crusades. Carmel was Mary's possession, her fief, and the Carmelites were the family in which her control was unquestioned. Everything is distilled into one traditional saying: "Carmel is entirely Marian." Carmelites belonged to her and enjoyed her special protection.

But the Carmelite charism was to shape its own special kind of Marian devotion with the passage of time. The need for a deeper relationship with Mary grew as the Carmelites grew in devotion to her Son. Intimacy with Mary followed naturally from intimacy with her Son. Mary gradually came to be recognized more as a Mother to be imitated than as a patron, and her "servants" more as sons than as "vassals." Mary became known as "Mother of Carmel" and was loved with the tender and spontaneous devotion of her children.

Carmelite intimacy with Mary finally discovered in her the woman of faith, later honored with the title, "Sister in the faith." In fact, some simply called her "Carmelite"—in other words, "one of us!" Carmelites are "Brothers and Sisters of the Blessed Virgin Mary." This final flowering of Carmelite devotion to Mary is beautifully expressed in the words of John Paul II: "...In her faith we can therefore rightly find a kind of 'key' which unlocks for us the innermost reality of Mary."

Christ-Centered: The Carmelite Rule

The Rule is like a mosaic of scriptural texts and allusions. The primary task of the Carmelite is the lectio divina, being not just an invitation to scholarly research but also to prayerful listening and reflection on the word of God. "The sword of the Spirit, the word of God, must dwell in your mouths and hearts," the Rule recalls. Here the term "dwell" takes on its full biblical force of penetrating deeply into the heart.

The Rule also recalls in biblical language that "life on earth is warfare." It develops the theme with military imagery and uses the symbol of "clothing," borrowed from Paul, to designate a call to inner conversion or change of heart. Many of the early hermits came from the warlike generation of the Crusades, so the imagery of war and combat in the Rule spoke directly to them with its biblical references to "the belt of truth, the breastplate of righteousness, the shield of faith, the helmet of salvation, and the sword of the Spirit which is the word of God."

The Rule begins and ends with a reference to the person of Jesus. In the opening lines, there is an unmistakable allusion to chapter one of Hebrews: "Long ago, God spoke to our ancestors in many and various ways by the prophets, but in these last days he has spoken to us by a Son." In this way, the Rule is designed to help the Carmelite think biblically and so live freely and spontaneously "in allegiance to Jesus Christ," who alone gives meaning to the Scriptures.

Teresa of Avila and John of the Cross

Teresa of Avila set about reforming the Carmelite Order in sixteenth-century Spain. She looked back for inspiration to the "holy fathers on Mount Carmel, who in such great solitude and with such contempt of the world sought this treasure [prayer and contemplation], this precious pearl." John of the Cross aided Teresa greatly in her reform, with Mount Carmel figuring prominently in his writings. *The Ascent of Mount Carmel* is the title of one of his great spiritual classics. He prefaced it with a rough sketch of Mount Carmel itself, which in essence contains his whole spiritual teaching.

The work of Teresa of Avila and John of the Cross, among others, ensured that the Carmelite Order reformed successfully, and was able to spread throughout the whole world. Today, Carmel encircles the globe and its spirit lives clothed in a rich variety of cultures. It is particularly through Thérèse of Lisieux that we can see the message of Carmel transmitted untainted and embodied faithfully for all to follow.

Thérèse: Sister in the Faith

When we examine the life of Thérèse, we can see how the Carmelite Order's founding, Rule, and beliefs permeated throughout. She echoed Elijah's perseverance in prayer when she said in her autobiography, *The Story of a Soul*, in her own moment of darkness: "I never ceased hoping against hope." She was to experience the still, small voice of God on her confirmation day. She wrote: "I did not experience an impetuous wind at the moment of the Holy Spirit's descent, but rather this light breeze which the prophet Elijah heard on Mount Horeb."

Thérèse wanted more of that spirit to be upon her.

She wrote: "I thought of the prayer Elisha made to our father Elijah, when he asked him for a double portion of his spirit." That prayer was to be answered in her life. Elijah's refrain: "I am zealous with zeal for the Lord God of hosts," has become the Carmelite motto. Thérèse's restless ambition to be everything in the Church—warrior, priest, apostle, doctor, martyr—certainly displays this zeal! Yet she displayed a tender devotion to Mary, referring to her as "...more mother than queen" and "...the example of the soul searching for Jesus in the night of faith."

When we reflect on the Carmelite Rule, we see how Thérèse fully lived out its every word. The lectio divina meant that Thérèse was called to an ever deeper intimacy with the Word as a unique place of encounter with God. She responded fully. She wrote, "The Gospels are enough," and would herself be described later as a "word" of God.

She also responded to the imagery of war and combat in the Rule. Nobody would wage war more relentlessly on her own selfishness: "I want to love like a little child," she said. "I want to fight like a valiant warrior. I will enter Carmel if I have to do so at the edge of a sword." She would even play the role of Joan of Arc in a community play, and this warrior heroine was one of her favorite models.

Thérèse also took inspiration from the two great reformers, Teresa of Avila and John of the Cross. On one occasion she said, "I want to become a saint. I want to love God as much as St. Teresa did." Her writings are littered with quotations from John's prose and poetry. "At the ages of seventeen and eighteen," she confessed, "I had no other spiritual nourishment."

The inner core of prayer and contemplation, at the heart of the Carmelite Rule, was to be Thérèse's driving force. She fully embraced the Rule in her desire to imitate Jesus more closely by a hidden life of prayer and sacrifice, and so entered the solitude of the French Carmel of Lisieux. "Carmel was the desert," she said, "where God wanted me to hide." Her example invites us to discover her "Little Way," and to please God by simply offering him, as Thérèse did, our "poor little actions and desires."

❧

Reflections

Where Your Treasure Is

Read 1 Kings 18:36–39

Only God can satisfy the deepest longings of the human heart; everything else is a false god. Yet there are still many empty idols in our lives. Some we are aware of, others we are not. Be honest and acknowledge this. Think specifically of one of your Baals—food, drink, work, a relationship, reputation, status, profit, efficiency, popularity—and reflect for a moment. Add to this anything else that you feel is an idol in your life. Name it. Now listen again to the challenge of Elijah: "How long will you hobble first on one leg, then on another? If Yahweh is God, follow him." There can be no compromise. Pray constantly that you may see the idols hidden within you. Ask for help to end the conflict. Above all, persevere in prayer.

Withdraw to Be Alone with God

Read 1 Kings 19:9–18

Choose a quiet place. Be calm. Let everything fall away—cares, anxieties, plans... Journey inward...slowly, slowly...deeper, deeper into your heart. At this moment God is not in the noise, the bustle, the rat-race, the wind, the fire, or the earthquake. Remain in the stillness...five, ten, fifteen minutes.... Let God act. Listen intently. The still, small voice speaks in the silence...it is the whisper of a gentle breeze.

Feeling Drained and Empty

Read 1 Kings 19:4–8

We all feel confusion, doubt, disappointment, loneliness, rejection, and failure at various times. What's the good of all the prayers we've said, the "great" work we've done for God, we moan. We are experiencing what Elijah did: "I've had enough. Take my life." Think back. Search. Find parallels in your life to his. Take one experience from which you have emerged not broken but renewed. How do you feel about it now that the storm has passed? It wasn't a breakdown, rather, a breakthrough, a blessing in disguise, new vision, new life. God was there in the void, the emptiness, the despair, the injustice, the bereavement, the opposition, the jealousy, the desertion, the betrayal of trust, the illness. God is still there changing you within, transforming you in this desert experience. He's hidden, so at times it's painful. It's like the pangs of a new birth. But be patient. Give God time. Let him transform you in the darkness.

Prayer

Song of Gratitude to Our Lady of Mount Carmel

Close to you, O my loving Mother!
I've found rest for my heart.
I want nothing more on earth.
Jesus alone is all my happiness.
If sometimes I feel sadness
And fear coming to assail me,
Always supporting me in my weakness,
Mother, you deign to bless me.

Grant that I may be faithful
To my divine Spouse Jesus.
One day may his sweet voice call me
To fly away among the elect.
Then, no more exile, no more suffering.
In Heaven I'll keep repeating
The song of my gratitude,
Loveable Queen of Carmel!

2

A Saint for Our Season

THERE IS A STORY ABOUT an American philosopher who went to Japan for a conference on religion. He overheard another American delegate saying to a Shinto priest: "We've now been to a good many of your ceremonies, and have seen quite a few of your shrines, but I don't get your ideology; I don't get your theology." The Japanese paused as though in deep thought and then slowly shook his head. "We don't have an ideology," he said, "we don't have a theology. We dance!" Thérèse could have said the same thing of her own life. She sings of God's merciful love, and she invites us to dance with her in response to that love.

Beginnings

Marie Françoise Thérèse Martin was born on January 2, 1873, in Alençon, a small town in Normandy, France. Her parents, Louis and Zelie, had four other girls: Marie, Pauline, Leonie, and Celine. (Two boys and two girls had already died in infancy.) Louis Martin was a watchmaker and jeweler by trade; Zelie had a thriving lace-making business.

Thérèse was baptized on January 4, and her eldest sister, Marie, was her godmother. At two weeks old, she almost died. At three months, she suffered further serious trouble with her health, but, fortunately, Thérèse survived. She was entrusted to a friendly nurse with whom she lived in the country for the next twelve months. She then returned to the warmth of the family home, and was a playful, high-spirited, and happy child.

When Thérèse was four years old, tragedy struck. Her mother, Zelie, died. Thérèse witnessed the final anointing and later would recall the last, cold kiss and the bare coffin. Afterward, the family moved to "Les Buissonets" in Lisieux. Thérèse had changed into a shy, quiet, and over-sensitive child. "A look was enough to reduce me to tears," she said. "I could not bear the company of strangers." After her mother's death, Thérèse had understandably grown extremely close to her father, so having to spend five years as a boarder at the Benedictine Abbey school in Lisieux made them "the saddest years" of her life, she later recalled.

She was devastated still further when her sister, Pauline, entered the Lisieux Carmel. At ten years of age, Thérèse once again became seriously ill. She suffered from nervous trembling and hallucinations. Her illness lasted almost two months before she was cured by Mary, who smiled at her, she said. Shortly before her death, in her last poem, she wrote: "You who came to smile at me in the

morning of my life, come smile at me again...
Mother...it is evening now."

A crisis of scruples later began which was to
last for over a year. Her eldest sister, Marie, also
entered the Lisieux Carmel, and her other sister,
Leonie, the Visitation Convent at Caen. Her torment was to end, however, on Christmas Eve, 1886,
when she was thirteen years old. Just like Elijah,
she experienced her own profound conversion. Her
childhood and childishness were left behind on this
"night of illumination" as "God filled my darkness
with a flood of light...I received the grace of my
complete conversion." Jesus had truly changed her
heart; she was no longer the peevish, whining child
but discovered her own identity and found
strength to face reality as never before.

Two years later, at the age of fourteen, this once
painfully shy girl actually had the courage to ask
Pope Leo XIII personally for permission to join her
two sisters in the Lisieux Carmel after her Bishop
had refused her request. After a month's prepara-
tion—"one of the most beautiful months of my
life," as she was to call it—she entered the Lisieux
Carmel on April 9, 1888, at the age of fifteen.

Life at Carmel

Thus, a new stage in her life began. "I am here forever," she said. Life wasn't without its trials, however. Her superior, Mother Marie de Gonzague, was
an aristocrat with charismatic charm and
qualities of greatness, but capricious and of an

uncertain, even volatile temperament. She recognized a treasure in Thérèse, but was not afraid to humiliate her. Thérèse didn't always find community life easy, and was subjected to some hurtful remarks that she shrugged off as "pinpricks." For example, her embroidering was clumsy, so she was called "the big nanny goat," and her deference to authority earned her the nickname of "Sister Amen."

While she was completing her first year's training, her father became mentally ill. Town gossip blamed this on his daughter's untimely entrance into the convent, and this was a severe trial for Thérèse. However, he recovered temporarily and she was able to walk down the aisle of the chapel on his arm to be clothed in the Carmelite habit. She pronounced her vows at seventeen, but not without first experiencing severe doubts about her vocation. At twenty, she assisted in the formation of the new arrivals to the community—among them were her own sister, Celine, and a cousin.

Gradually, Thérèse settled into community life, enjoying painting pictures, composing poems, and writing plays. Her natural wit began to emerge. She wasn't afraid to laugh, having a large repertoire of tricks and jokes about herself and others, and being a great mimic. Her superior once described her like this: "She is filled with tricks...a mystic, a comedienne...she can make you shed tears of devotion; and she can just as easily make you split your sides with laughter." She almost went to heaven when, playing Joan of Arc in a play she had written, the straw at the stake caught fire.

Her mischievous spirit saved her from taking herself too seriously, even daring her to challenge the rigid conventions of holiness and the strict regulations in her own family and in her adopted family of Carmel. For example, one Sister strongly opposed the "Martin clan" and voiced her support of the superior's disciplinarian treatment of Thérèse's sister, Celine. "Mother Gonzague has every right to test her," she said. "Why be surprised about it?" A firm voice rose against this: "There are some trials which one does not have the right to impose," Thérèse replied. When she felt particularly hemmed in by rigidly interpreted Church laws and regulations, which restricted the reception of the Eucharist, she never hesitated to voice her disapproval. "I understood that the Church had a heart," she explained, "that this heart was burning with love." But the Church's heart could be concealed and lost sight of with undue emphasis on legalism and control. It is this heart of love that keeps the Church throbbing with life, makes reform possible, and puts everything in perspective.

Thérèse's humor was always gentle and kind, not unlike the humor of the Gospels, sending little ripples across the mind and releasing tensions. It was to mask her constant inner struggle against "thickest darkness," especially at the end of her life. On Holy Thursday 1896, the day after she had made a formal offering of herself to God's merciful love, she had her first hemorrhage. Tuberculosis was to ravage her body. Yet even in the final stages of her illness, the sparkle was present. She described the consumption wasting her frail body with a light touch: "I cough and cough and cough," she said, "like an old train coming into the station." She looked at photos of the two missionary priests entrusted to her prayers and said, "I'm better looking myself than either of them!" On one occasion, three of the Sisters kept vigil at her bedside and fell asleep. As they woke up again she looked at each of them in turn and said, "Peter, James, and John." She saddled her doctor with the nickname "Clodion the Hairy," after a fifth-century Frankish chief. Her cousin described her at this time as "cheerfulness itself" and commented: "She is always making those who come to visit her laugh. There are times when one would pay to be near her. I believe she will die laughing, she is so happy." Little wonder that the martyr Theophane Venard was one of her special favorites: "O Theophane," she wrote, "you lived and died with a smile."

Her humor does not make her any less of a spiritual genius nor does it minimize the deep knowledge of God which she experienced through love from her earliest years. It makes her an even more attractive witness to the power of God's action, which does not destroy our natural gifts and talents but allows them to develop freely, spontaneously, easily. Thérèse gave holiness a new look with her laughter; it was stamped with an original touch. She was highly graced by God, but she too had to grow in grace, in age, and in wisdom. Like Jesus, she was fully human, fully alive.

No one insisted more than she did on the uncompromising and radical demands of love. Thérèse understood that God is no universal policeman, meticulous accountant, powerful law-giver, or perfectionist. She was totally in tune with the playfulness of God. For Thérèse, God was fun to be with; generosity and joy were the unmistakable signs of his presence.

Lessons from Thérèse's Life

On September 30, 1897, at the age of twenty-four, Thérèse died, eighteen months after the first symptoms of tuberculosis had appeared. What relevance can a twenty-four-year-old French nun have in today's changing Church, a Church so unlike the one she knew? Can we really expect much from this young woman brought up in a narrow, rigid family environment, highly conditioned by her French culture, apparently quite neurotic, hidden away for several years in an enclosed Carmelite convent, practically unrecognized within her own community, and who died unknown to the world at large? No less a theologian of the modern Church than Karl Rahner found Thérèse "irritating," "boring," and "repulsive."

It is true that her language does often ring soft and sentimental. But this is part of her challenge; she is not just writing for and communicating with the spiritual elite. Everyone can find a deep pool of inspiration in her writings. Thérèse does not have a theology, she does not have an ideology; she simply talks to us, sharing with us her own experience of living, of dying, of what it means to be frail and fully human. She is a person of real flesh and blood. Temperament, language, and culture must not be allowed to conceal the real woman from us or to obscure her message. Thérèse gives us a whole new approach to God, a Gospel vision rediscovered. She gives consolation, hope, and renewed courage to anguished minds and hearts everywhere. But she must be allowed to speak for herself in her own way, not with arguments, not with proofs, but with the burning witness of her own life and death.

Thérèse's courage in facing difficult decisions and situations is an obvious example of a lesson we can learn from her. As a young religious, Thérèse became uneasy in her relations with another Sister, and felt that she must act in love to ensure a more honest way of sharing, no matter what the cost. "The time had come," she said, "and I must no longer fear to speak out...I told her everything I was thinking about her." She explained later, "If I'm not loved, that's just too bad. I tell the truth, and if anyone doesn't wish to know the truth let her not come looking for me." Someone once begged her to say a few "edifying" words to her doctor. She replied that he could think whatever he wanted of her: "I love only simplicity; I have a horror of pretence." She would say on her deathbed: "I have never sought anything but the truth."

To avoid the challenge of speaking out in love is the easy option. Thérèse knew this. She admitted that criticism of this kind is "a painful operation," but she added, "truth always wins out." Much time and energy can be wasted pushing the Church to change. Thérèse has her own lesson for loyal dissidents: love the Church into change.

Thérèse is able to voice the hurt of many women who feel excluded by the Church today. Hers is not a strident voice, but a plaintive one. She challenged the Church she loved so deeply. She recalled how she traveled in Italy as a young girl. "But every moment," she said, "someone was saying: 'Don't enter here! Don't enter there! You'll be excommunicated!'" In desperation, she released her indignation:

> Ah, poor women, how they are misunderstood! And yet they love God in much larger numbers than men do, and during the passion of Our Lord, women had more courage than the Apostles since they braved the insults of the soldiers and dared to dry the adorable face of Jesus. It is undoubtedly because of this that he allows misunderstandings to be their lot on earth, since he chose it for himself. In heaven, he will show that his thoughts are not men's thoughts, for then the first shall be last.

Thérèse had always had an ardent desire to be a priest, which is especially relevant today in the light of Pope John Paul II's letter on the vocation of women, *Mulieris Dignitatem*. Her words—"I feel the vocation of the warrior, the priest, the apostle, the doctor, the martyr"—have sparked much controversy. Thérèse is not a champion of "women priests"; rather, she is a champion of the truth. Nobody will affirm her fidelity to the teaching of the Church better than she, in the true Carmelite tradition. She makes the words of Carmel's reformer, Teresa of Avila, her own: "I want to be a daughter of the Church." Thérèse's desire to be a priest is expressed clearly in the context of her vocation to give her all to be love at the heart of the Church. Celine, her sister, recalled how Thérèse, when she knew she was seriously ill, said: "You see, God is going to take me at an age when I would not have had the time to become a priest. If I could have been a priest, I would have been ordained at the June ordination. How different things would be in heaven," Thérèse mused.

We are also shown by Thérèse how we don't have to do extraordinary things to be loved by or to love God. At that time, there was great debate over whether holiness consisted of heroic deeds, extraordinary penances, ecstasies, and visions (as the Jansenists believed), or whether by faith alone. Thérèse never minimized the importance of "works." "The most beautiful thoughts are nothing without works," she tells us.

But mighty deeds as such held no attraction for her. A few weeks before Thérèse's death, a member of the community said: "She's a sweet little Sister, but what will we be able to say about her after her death? She didn't do anything." But sanctity does not consist in stunning deeds or great achievements. The ordinary is extraordinary enough. Thérèse understood the scandal of the Incarnation: "Where did this man get this wisdom and these mighty works? Is not this the carpenter's son?" "Living on love," she said, "is not setting up one's tent on the top of Tabor." Thérèse's way is firmly rooted in the humdrum.

I once saw an exhibition of Picasso's works. In the distance, my eye caught the antlers of a deer. I approached the sculpture to look at it more closely. The artist had taken the discarded handlebars of a bicycle, turned them upside down, and thus transformed and shaped them into a work of art. Like Thérèse, he saw the potential in the most insignificant, commonplace, and ordinary item. This is what she stresses: God is in the ordinary, the insignificant, the here and now. God is everywhere, in everything. Holiness can be found in the workplace, the grind of daily living, schools, hospitals, the kitchen sink. Her God—our God—walks among the computers and the pots and the pans. He works in the chaos of life, its confusion and mess, giving shape to the meaningless and creating beauty out of nothing.

Thérèse took as her inspiration the Gospel message: "Love one another as I have loved you." She lived this commandment to the full, despite it being a great challenge to her—as, indeed, it is for us all. But more importantly, for her and for us, she discovered that this is not just a commandment—it is a gift. Jesus does not merely require us to love like him; Jesus himself does it for us! Jesus, she said, "loves others in me.... For me to love you as you love, I would have to borrow your own love."

Her greatness lies not in what she said, or did, or wrote, but in the fact that the Holy Spirit found in her an open heart. She found greatness in surrendering to the Spirit's transforming touch.

We can all be quick to judge. But Thérèse reminds us that "the Artist of souls is happy when we don't stop at the outward shows, but penetrate into the inner sanctuary where he chooses to dwell, and admire its beauty." One little story illustrates this well. A member of the community seemed to cause Thérèse many struggles, but she was always careful to respond with love and greet her constantly with a friendly smile. The Sister became convinced that she was Thérèse's special favorite and wondered at the attraction. "What attracted me," said Thérèse, "was Jesus hidden in the depths of her soul." It would be a mistake to conclude that Thérèse first saw Jesus in this Sister and then loved her. She didn't. Jesus was hidden, concealed from her by human weakness. She only saw a weak, frail, and broken human person who irked and irritated her, and tested her patience beyond human limits. But a familiar truth was dawning more deeply on her: "forgive us...as we forgive." She had reached out in mercy to human weakness in another and Jesus revealed himself to her in response to her love. He was there at work all the time—unseen!—behind the human veil.

Thérèse was plunged into a sinful, self-destructive world of unbelief not to condemn it, but to understand and reach out to it. It took missionary grace to be able to become a "companion," in the literal sense of "one who shares bread" with someone else, of unbelievers. She spoke of "sitting at the table of unbelievers...at the table full of bitterness...sharing their bread of pain...." Later, she called them "brothers." This was not just their darkness, it was hers. "I run toward Jesus," she said, "and ask him to open eternity to the poor unbelievers." She didn't utter a word of complaint, rather: "The Lord sent me this trial when I had the strength to bear it." Thérèse's perseverance, her hope, got her through the darkness. "My kind of madness is to hope," she said.

We live in a time of great upheaval, challenge, and change. Thérèse is able to help us with her "way of trust and absolute surrender" to face the future and stumble confidently across the threshold of the third millennium. We can look to Thérèse, in whom love burned as fire, and instead of cursing the darkness, kindle a light. Thérèse's mission lives on in us today: "I will spend my heaven doing good upon earth." As she so eloquently put it, in the words of the Gospel: "I have come to cast fire on the earth and how I wish it were blazing already."

Reflections

Our God Dances

Read Zephaniah 3:14–18

Does this image of God surprise you? Reflect on it for a moment and ponder your reaction. It is a truth that can change your life. Think of some ways in which it can. Many people live by rules alone; it's a kind of security. To observe the law is to be holy, they feel. But God is not a policeman, an accountant, a lawgiver, or a perfectionist. He is not rigid, inflexible, or calculating. He wants us to enjoy life, to love life, and to be happy—not to be gloomy, sour-faced followers of his Son. God is fun to be with, a joy! He invites us to discover our inner spring of joy. Thérèse was in touch with her inner spring, even in the thickest darkness. God is this inner spring of joy. To be joyful is to be godlike. To be holy is to dance with God. Ponder on how you can adjust your life to fit this image of a dancing God. Persevere in silent prayer.

The Sacrament of the Present Moment

Read Exodus 3:13–15

I was regretting the past and fearing the future. Suddenly my Lord was speaking:

"My NAME is I AM."

He paused. I waited. He continued.

"When you live in the past with its mistakes and regrets, it's hard. I am not there. My name is not I was. When you live in the future, with its problems and fears, it's hard. I am not there. My name is not I will be.

"When you live at this moment, it's not hard. I am here.

"My NAME is I AM."

(Helen Mallicoat)

The Impossible Commandment

Read John 13:34–35; 15:12–13

Think of someone with whom you find it difficult to relate, someone who irritates you, rubs you the wrong way, or tests your patience constantly—even, at times, beyond your human limits, as Thérèse experienced. Reflect for a moment. I don't have to see Jesus at work in this person. He is there, working silently, imperceptibly, delicately, hidden. I believe he's there: that's the difference. I can see only a real person—weak, frail, broken, just like myself, in fact. Let yourself love...love and you will discover the hidden Jesus; or, rather, he will reveal himself to you from his hiding place. It's his response to your love. By loving, we discover love. "Lord, when did we see you hungry...thirsty...a stranger...naked...sick...in prison?" If we need to ask, we're not seeing Jesus!

Ah! Lord, I know you don't command the impossible. You know better than I do my weakness and imperfection; you know very well that never would I be able to love my Sisters as you love them, unless you, O my Jesus, loved them in me. It is because you wanted to give me this grace that you made your new commandment. Oh! How I love this new commandment since it gives me the assurance that your will is to love in me all those you command me to love! Yes, I feel it, when I am charitable, it is Jesus alone who is acting in me, and the more united I am to him, the more do I love my Sisters.

Prayer

Living on Love!...

On the evening of Love, speaking without parable,
Jesus said: "If anyone wishes to love me
All his life, let him keep my Word.
My Father and I will come to visit him
And we will make his heart our dwelling.
Coming to him, we shall love him always.
We want him to remain, filled with peace,
In our Love!...
Living on Love is holding You Yourself.
Uncreated Word, Word of my God,
Ah! Divine Jesus, you know I love you.
The Spirit of Love sets me aflame with his fire.
In loving you I attract the Father.
My weak heart holds him forever.
O Trinity! You are Prisoner
Of my Love!...

3

Jesus: My Only Love!

THE JESUS THÉRÈSE DISCOVERED in the Gospels recalls a story about Thorwalden's statue of Christ. The artist set himself to make the finest statue ever. Time passed and eventually he was ready to give the world his masterpiece. It was strong, imposing, and striking. The head was thrown back defiantly; the arms were raised in a gesture of command. But, at night, fog and mist rose from the sea before the clay could fully harden. The statue sagged, the head drooped gently, the arms rested, the lips curled, the eyes softened. It was no longer a commanding figure. It still had great power and strength, but now it had compassion, too, and tenderness, gentleness. It was the same statue, but changed completely—a total transformation. It displayed strength fused with weakness. At first Thorwalden was disappointed. But then it slowly dawned on him: here was unbounded love appealing through human weakness and reaching out to weakness in others. The experience had given him the merciful Jesus of the Gospels. So he called the statue "Learn of me."

This is the Jesus Thérèse discovered in the Gospels: fully alive, fully human, tender, and compassionate. "The bruised reed he will not break, the smoldering flax he will not quench" (Isaiah 42:3). Jesus invites everyone to learn of him. But first he exclaims, "I give you thanks, Lord of heaven and earth, because you have concealed these things from the wise and prudent and revealed them to little ones" (Matthew 11:25). What are the "things" God has concealed from the learned and the clever and revealed to little ones? Thérèse provided her own answer: "Because I was little and weak," she said, "he instructed me in the things of love. These are the secrets hidden from the learned, and to possess them one has to be poor in spirit...the yoke of the Lord is sweet and light; it is only love that can expand my heart." Thérèse discovered in Jesus the secret of God's love.

In this Jesus of the Gospels, she discovered not only the power and strength of God, but also the weakness of God. In him, she discovered her own weakness too. She recalled the invitation of Jesus again. This time it inspired a description of what she called the greatest grace of her life: "I prefer to own in all simplicity that he who is mighty has done great things for me, and the greatest of these is that he has shown me my own littleness and how incapable I am of anything good." Thérèse unveiled the heart of Jesus. He is tender and brittle, "meek and humble." In him, she also learned the lesson of her own weakness: "When I am weak then I am strong."

Thérèse was deeply conscious of her weakness, but never daunted by it. For her, weakness wasn't an obstacle to intimacy with God; rather, it was a steppingstone: "If you are willing to bear serenely the trial of being displeasing to yourself, then you will be for Jesus a pleasant place of shelter."

Scott Peck, in his best-selling inspirational book, *The Road Less Traveled,* picks up her words again to help him define a true Christian. Her way of weakness and humble self-acceptance is surely the road less traveled. Like so many others, she was familiar with classics of the spiritual life such as *The Way of Perfection.* But this kind of "perfectionist" language seems to suggest that everything is possible by our own efforts. It isn't. We need redemption both individually and collectively as Church. Thérèse saw this more clearly than most. Her way of imperfection has a much more authentic and evangelical ring about it.

As we grow older, we seem to grow weaker and often more deeply conscious of our sins, our faults, and our failings; indeed, we are ever more fragile. Thérèse felt the same: "In the early days," she said, "I used to wonder what further heights there could be for me to climb. But, of course, I realized before long that the further you go along the road the more conscious you are of the distance between you and the goal; and by now—well, by now I'm resigned to seeing myself always far from perfect." Her final sentence has a kind of impish humor. I can see her smiling, winking as she wrote: "I'm even glad of it in a way." At ease with her own limitations! It's certainly an original comment on spiritual maturity.

This experience of her own weakness drove Thérèse to the Gospels. There she discovered a Jesus who was weak, frail, brittle, and human like herself; and above all passionately in need of love. In one of Thérèse's favorite Gospel scenes, Jesus sleeps through a storm; in another, he stops to rest by Jacob's well, tired and thirsty. She needed a God like this—weak, little, needy, human. She could walk with this Jesus at her side. The Word became weakness for her. He was the human face of God, the mysterious meeting-place with God, at one with her in the messiness of daily living. He experienced all her deepest human needs. He shared her weakness and her need for love.

The extract below is from one of her poems, addressed to Jesus as "The Only Friend Whom I Love":

> I need a heart burning with tenderness,
> to be my support forever,
> to love everything in me, even my weakness,
> and never to leave me day or night.
> I must have a God who takes on my nature
> and becomes my brother and is able to suffer!

A Thirst for Love

The Jesus of Thérèse is unbounded love appealing through human weakness. He draws everyone to himself. He hangs on the cross with open arms outstretched in love and says, "I thirst." Thérèse observed: "I seemed to hear Jesus say to me what he said to the Samaritan woman: "Give me to drink!"" (John 4:7). She saw how he took the initiative and begged a little water from a sinful woman. She commented: "It was the love of his poor creature the Creator of the universe was seeking." He was thirsty, she said, "for love." She explained: "Jesus is parched, because he finds few hearts who surrender to him without reservations, who understand the real tenderness of his infinite Love." All the tenderness of his heart was there for Thérèse in his parched cry from the cross: "I thirst."

Thérèse herself became one with this thirst of Jesus: "I slaked his thirst and the more I gave him to drink, the more the thirst of my poor little soul increased. It was this ardent thirst he was giving me as the most delightful drink of his love." One Sunday she saw a picture of Our Lord on the cross. She was deeply moved: "I was resolved to remain in spirit at the foot of the cross," she said. "The cry of Jesus on the cross sounded continually in my heart: 'I thirst.' These words ignited within me an unknown and very living fire. I wanted to give my Beloved to drink and I felt myself consumed with a thirst for souls."

It is hardly surprising that Mary Magdalene was one of her favorite Gospel characters—a woman like herself, who was fired with a passionate love for Jesus and was not afraid to take risks in search of his love. "Most of all I imitate the conduct of the Magdalene," she said, "her astonishing or rather her loving audacity which charms the heart of Jesus. Yes, I feel it."

Thérèse identified totally with Mary Magdalene in her search. Her quest throbbed with a passionate intensity like hers. He was "her" Jesus, and she too wants "to take him in her arms and carry him away." Like the spouse in the Song of Songs, she lingered with Mary Magdalene, weeping, looking for the One she loves. The consolations of the sympathetic angels at the tomb leave them both indifferent. Nothing in creation can satisfy their longings for their absent Jesus. In one of her poems she identifies with Mary Magdalene's cry: "Bright nature, if I do not see God, you are nothing to me but a vast tomb." The more Thérèse discovered Jesus the more she discovered that she had yet to discover more about him; and her confidence and her love for him increased all the more. At last, she discovered, like the Magdalene, that she "cannot vanquish him in love."

On the lintel of the door of her room, Thérèse engraved these words: "Jesus is my only love." They provided the original title for one of her poems, "Jesus Alone." It is a love song where once again we recognize Thérèse as the great, passionate lover of

Jesus: "You want my heart, Jesus, I give it to you. I surrender all my desires to you." Everything impelled her to the person of Jesus. St. John never tired of repeating that "God is love." But Thérèse never used the phrase. For her, it had to be still more focused. Jesus is love, Jesus alone! Her whole life was a love-relationship with a person. He was her friend, beloved, companion, brother, even thief. He was not an idea, nor an abstraction. He was warm, tender, and human—a person of flesh and blood. He was everything, "my only love."

Thérèse wanted to love Jesus beyond laws and limits, "unto folly." Her great patroness, Teresa of Avila, once said: "There are some, Lord, who serve you better than I, but that there should be some who love you more, or more ardently desire your glory, I will never abide!" One incident illustrates how much Thérèse had made these words her own. She once confided to her confessor: "Father, I want to become a saint; I want to love God as much as St. Teresa did." The Jesuit tried to moderate the aspirations of his penitent. She replied: "But, Father, I do not think that these are rash desires since Our Lord said, 'Be perfect as your heavenly Father is perfect.'" Thérèse did not want to be "perfect" by any strict or rigid observance of laws and regulations. She wanted to be "perfect" in the Gospel sense: to release the full potential of her love for Jesus.

We see Thérèse's quest for love in her language. She addressed God the Father like this: "You so loved me that you gave your only Son to be my

Savior and my Spouse." She often spoke of Jesus as her "Spouse." She addressed him in her prayer as "My Beloved Spouse." She would not be outdone in generosity even by her cousin's wedding invitation: "I learned from her example," she said, "concerning the delicate attentions a bride can bestow on her bridegroom." On behalf of her father who was seriously ill Thérèse, too, wrote her own invitation and addressed it to all of those invited to her wedding: "To have you take part in the marriage of his daughter, Thérèse, with Jesus, the Word of God." Here, too, we see her originality. And yet, to be the consecrated bride of Christ was not for her the summit of the spiritual life. For Thérèse, union with Jesus— described by Teresa of Avila in its highest stage as the spiritual marriage—was essentially the baptismal relationship of *every* believer. "The heart of my Spouse is mine alone just as mine is his alone." The whole venture of faith was a loving quest for closer intimacy with her Jesus, her only love.

Strength Through Weakness, Love from Pain

Thérèse longed to be identified more and more with the weakness of Jesus. She had just one simple aspiration: "Jesus, make me resemble you." This deep longing led her inexorably to the Passion. There she was to plunge even more deeply into the mystery of love revealed in human weakness. She described her first real meeting with a suffering Savior long before she entered Carmel: "The first sermon I understood was a sermon on the Passion," she said. But she was to discover the Passion again later, in a strange and entirely new way—in the face of Jesus.

Devotion to the Holy Face was a particularly popular devotion of the day. At first it had no special appeal for Thérèse, but her discovery of it was to coincide significantly with the mysterious mental illness of her father, who had always been for Thérèse the image of God's love. That image now gave way to the image of her father as a man of sorrows: "I had never before fathomed the depths of the treasures hidden in the Holy Face," she said. Her ability to see God's love through pain and suffering is another lesson from Thérèse that all of us can begin to appreciate. Perhaps it is her special gift to the children of today's dysfunctional families who cannot relate to the image of God as a loving Father, but who can relate to "the Man of Sorrows."

It was through the Servant Songs of Isaiah that Thérèse really entered deeply into the mystery of love hidden and revealed in human weakness: "...there is no beauty in him... no comeliness..." She confided, "These words of Isaiah have been the whole foundation of my devotion to the Holy Face, or to express it better, the foundation of my whole piety." She would not soften in any way the impact of the prophet's words on her own life: "I desired that like the Face of Jesus, my face be truly hidden, that no one on earth should know me. I thirsted to be forgotten...I also have desired to be without beauty, to tread the winepress alone, unknown to every creature." Even on her deathbed, she recited phrases from the Servant Songs.

Thérèse had chosen a life hidden away, unrecognized by the world, a life which she believed was her calling from God and wholly pleasing to him. She embarked on a way of total self-giving love. Far from escaping or avoiding human weakness with all its human pain, she embraced a life of sacrifice and prayer with love. She found her model in the Suffering Servant—forgotten, hidden, and unknown. Sacrifice is not a denial of joy; it is love in action. Thérèse longed passionately to empty herself totally, even of merits, but only to make space for love: "In the evening of life I shall stand before you with empty hands."

It's easy to attribute all these desires to be hidden, forgotten, despised, trodden underfoot as she said, like a grain of sand, to neurosis—an urge to escape from the challenges of life and its pain. But it wasn't like this. Thérèse could say to us in the words of Garth Brook's song: "I might have missed the pain, but I would have missed the dance."

A poem by Thérèse beautifully expresses her desire to remove all the layers of selfishness and to be stripped of everything for love of Jesus:

> For You, I've strewn my life
> my future, with what's gone:
> To mortal eye
> A rose that always will be withered from now
>   on,
> I ought to die!

This image of "an unpetalled rose" may appear quite trite for us today, but for Thérèse the reality it spoke of is absolute self-giving—generous, unreserved, hidden, and unknown. It was her total response to love revealed to her in what she called the "Beauty Supreme" of the Suffering Servant: "I don't want to give in order to receive." This love is never satisfied. Her life in Carmel would indeed pass unnoticed by the world, but, like the face of the Suffering Servant, it would be a thing of beauty, a mystery of love—in God's eyes, beyond price.

Perhaps the most consoling teaching of Thérèse about suffering is to assure us that we do not have to bear it heroically, or even courageously. She tells us "to carry our crosses weakly...let us suffer feebly and without courage." But she teaches us to do much more than just accept passively the inevitable weakness and pain of the human condition. She invites us to turn it into a way of loving. We can do much more than just put up with death; we can, in fact, transform it. Every kind of human weakness can be transfigured by trust and love. Thérèse desired what Jesus desired—the unfolding of God's plan of love for his people through suffering, and her place with him through her suffering in the redemption of the world.

In the infirmary where Thérèse lived out her final agony, there was a fresco on a wall that represented Jesus in Gethsemane. He is accepting the cup of suffering offered to him by the angel and is devastated by fear. He looks for comfort from friends and an escape from his anguish. He finds neither: "Let this chalice pass." Jesus accepted the pain and suffering—sorrow, confusion, fear, loneliness—that are part of human weakness, but he had to struggle with them in the garden. He accepted fully the mystery of evil and suffering, and in it he surrendered to the mystery of love: "Abba, Father, thy will be done."

Near the end of her life, Thérèse's darkness deepened as well: "The trial that faces me makes me shudder," she said. "I'm in the garden of agony and the prayer of Our Lord bursts from my heart at every moment." She experienced the "dread" of Jesus in Gethsemane: "Why should I be protected more than anyone else from the fear of death?" she said. She certainly knew the fear of dying, but there was never any denial of fear. Thérèse, too, was to struggle in the end like Jesus in the garden and to plumb the depths of human weakness: "This is really the agony with no consolation," she said. "My God, whatever you will but have pity on me. Have pity on me." She knew that she could not choose to suffer or not to suffer, to die or not to die, since it is all part of the human condition. But she knew that she could choose to love or not to love. Thérèse chose to love. Her deathbed conversation with her sister Celine illustrates this best of all: "What are you doing? You ought to try to sleep," Celine said. "I cannot. I am praying," Thérèse replied. "What are you saying to Jesus?" her sister asked. She replied: "I say nothing...I just love him."

The account of Thérèse's final moments reads like a description of the crucifixion:

> For more than two hours, a terrible rattle tore her chest. Her face was blue, her hands purplish, her feet were cold, and she shook in all her members. Perspiration stood out in enormous drops on her forehead and rolled down her cheeks. Her difficulties in breathing were always increasing.
>
> (Epilogue, *Story of a Soul,* p. 270)

Thérèse did not desire suffering like this any more than Jesus did on the cross. She recoiled from it, as he did. Two hours before her death, in total agony, she confided: "I would never have believed it possible to suffer so much! Never! Never! Never! I can only make sense of this in terms of my ardent desire to save souls."

Jesus died in abandonment and isolation: "My God, my God why have you forsaken me?" We don't know why, but through it he did plunge more deeply into the mystery of God's love. The pain is part of that mystery. "I assure you, the chalice is filled to the brim!" Thérèse said at the end, "but God is not going to abandon me, I'm sure...He has never abandoned me." Thérèse surrendered like Jesus to the mystery of pain in order to reach the even greater mystery of love.

Learn of Me

Read Matthew 11:25–30

The Niagara River explodes with energy as it dashes madly over the falls. This vast potential was wasted for millions of years, but is now harnessed. There is power and control, movement and restriction; a massive strength held in reserve. Think of other examples in the world around you: the powerful explosive forces held together by a tiny atom, the massive force of a river in spate channeled and restricted by its banks, a wild horse tamed by constant training....

Deep within us there are wild and unruly urges. Pause for a moment and acknowledge this, and listen to the words of Paul: "I do not understand my own behavior—the will to do what is good is in me, the power to do it is not: the good thing I want to do, I never do; the evil thing which I do not want—that is what I do" (Romans 7:19).

Pause and reflect. Jesus, help me. I cannot do it on my own. Save me from the evil that lies hidden in my heart, those uncontrolled impulses and unrestrained forces deep within me. Your call is not a call to weakness but to meekness: "When I am weak then I am strong...he was crucified in weakness, but lives by the power of God. We are weak in him, but we shall live with him by the power of God" (2 Corinthians 12:10; 13:4).

Jesus, you are calling me to be like you—meek and humble of heart. I let my heart reach out to you: Jesus, meek and humble of heart, make my heart like your heart. Stay with this aspiration; repeat it often. Be still. Persevere in prayer.

Like One Despised and Rejected

Read Isaiah 52:13—53:12

Choose a quiet place. Take a crucifix with you, and look at it for a moment. Consider the sufferings of Jesus: betrayal...desertion by his friends...rejection...denial...misunderstanding...loneliness...physical pain...injustice...mockery...death.... Find parallels in your own life and add them to the list. Try to discover a pattern in God's actions when you reflect on your own painful experiences.

God enters your heart through these wounds. Name your own wounds—grief, anxiety, failure, bereavement, a broken relationship... Take them with you before the Crucified. His ways are not our ways. On the cross Jesus is the power and the wisdom of God for the believer, but weakness and foolishness for many others—a stumbling block, a sign of contradiction. The foolishness of God is wiser than human wisdom and his weakness is stronger than human strength. He chooses the weak to shame the strong. He is calling us to be like him. His way is not always easy, but it is always his way. He knows best how to make us like his Son.

Stay in spirit at the foot of the cross. Persevere in silent prayer.

How I Want to Love

It's your love, Jesus, that I crave.
It's your love that has to transform me.
Put in my heart your consuming flame,
And I'll be able to bless you and love you.
Yes, I'll be able to love you and bless you
As they do in Heaven.
I'll love you with that very love
With which you have loved me, Jesus Eternal
   Word.

4

Like Little Children

THÉRÈSE HAD MANY favorite pictures of Jesus. In
one of them, given to her as a child, he is seated
with a little child who is climbing onto his lap and
hugging him innocently. But there is also another
child in the picture standing beside Jesus. Thérèse
spontaneously identified with the child clinging to
him: "The other little one does not appeal to me as
much," she said. "He is standing like an adult."
Underneath the picture are the words: "Let the little children come to me, do not stop them; for it is
to such as these that the kingdom of God belongs"
(Luke 18:16–17). Jesus was indignant with his disciples when he spoke these words. They had scold-
ed the people for bringing little children to him so
that he might touch them. But Jesus embraced the
little children, laid his hands upon them, and gave
them his blessing. He also used the occasion to
drive home an important lesson: "In truth I tell
you, anyone who does not welcome the kingdom of
God like a little child will never enter it."

The lesson of this scene was to mature and
develop significantly for her with the passing of
years and her reflection on the Gospels in the light

of her own experience. Like the disciples of Jesus, she too was later to ask herself: "Who is the greatest in the kingdom of heaven?" In answer to that same question, Jesus called a little child to himself and said: "The one who makes himself as little as this little child is the greatest in the kingdom of heaven" (Matthew 18:1–3). Then he distilled the whole significance of the scene into one weighty sentence: "I tell you solemnly, unless you change and become like little children, you will never enter the kingdom of heaven."

The Call to Conversion

Thérèse admitted that learned books left her dry and muddled, but that when she took the Gospels all seems clear: "A single word opens up infinite horizons." So, too, we can take Jesus' key words from the Gospels and let Thérèse comment on them with her own experience and insights. Her life and her words open up this saying in a remarkable way: its depth, its significance, its bearing on how we live and on how we die. It is a summary of her whole life and teaching.

Jesus challenges us to change if we want to become like little children. That's the condition. But when the Gospel speaks of change, it is not just speaking of some kind of external change, but it is a call to "conversion." It's asking us to change our minds and our way of looking at things. It is a challenge to alter our opinions—at times, even to admit we're wrong and say we're sorry—and to look again at something and to see it from a different angle. It is a challenge to openness. Conversion in the Gospel sense refers to an inner disposition or an attitude of mind and heart. St. Peter describes it well in the case of every woman: "Your beauty must lie, not in braided hair, not in gold trinkets, not in the dress you wear, but in the hidden features of your hearts, in a possession you can never lose, that of a calm and tranquil spirit, in God's eyes, beyond price" (1 Peter 3:3–4).

There was one important change in the life of Thérèse that could easily go unnoticed. She did not call it a "conversion," in fact, she never spoke about it. We only know of it from the profound impact it had on her life. We find only one reference to God's mercy in her writings before she wrote *The Story of a Soul.* When she wrote this autobiography just two years before her death, like so many of us, she seemed to have given God's mercy little more than some kind of notional assent. But something happened in her life that opened her heart to experience mercy in a new way. It was a conversion in the real Gospel sense, a profound change. There would be many other conversions in her life, deep and significant changes in her approach to God. But at some moment unknown to us (we cannot date her discovery of mercy) she discovered the great truth of God's mercy in such a way that she was now prepared to surrender her whole life to it—utterly, completely, entirely. It became everything for her. Conversion was to follow conversion, with struggle and pain and effort. Again, she does not refer to her experiences as conversions. They were just so many crucial moments or turning points in her long and painful process of growth. She knew that she was a child of God, but she had to discover for herself what it costs to "become" the child she already was and how the "impossible" really is possible, though not by her own efforts. We can trace this discovery at some of the important turning points in her life.

A Time for Love

Thérèse set herself to write the story of her soul, flushed with her great passion for God's mercy in obedience to her sister (who was then her superior). On the first page of her life story, Thérèse reflected on her calling. God's mercy opens up. "I'm going to do only one thing," she said, "I shall begin to sing what I must sing eternally: 'The Mercies of the Lord.'" Thérèse invites everyone to make the same discovery of God's mercy that she made. She opened her heart to receive what she called "the waves of infinite tenderness," and promised to help everyone else to do the same. At the end of her life, she said that her mission to teach others "the way of trust and absolute surrender" to God's merciful love was about to begin.

Thérèse had said of her Christmas Eve conversion experience: "God was able in a very short time to extricate me from the very narrow circle in which I was turning without knowing how to come out." For Thérèse, it was God who then intervened to save her. He did everything; she was powerless.

This same pattern emerged again at other crucial moments in her life. Thérèse was to become a great saint, but she could so easily have become a scholar instead. She was still young when she spoke of her "intense desire to know things." "I had always loved the great and the beautiful," she said, "but at this epoch in my life I was taken up with an extreme desire for learning." Her young, nimble mind was expanding and was drinking in knowledge. She embarked with passion on the study of history and science: "In a few months I acquired more knowledge than during my years of study. I was at the most dangerous age for young girls." But God intervened to save her: "God did for me," she said, "what Ezekiel reports in his prophecies, 'Behold your time was the time of lovers.'" Thérèse was never to deny the value of learning. On the contrary; immediately after this, she said, "My thirst for knowledge grew." But now God revealed something new to her: love is the priority. We discover love by loving. The words of John take on deeper meaning: "He who loves knows God; he who does not love does not know God" (1 John 4:7–8). Again, he did everything. She was powerless. She explained this with a simple comment: "Yes, Jesus did all this for me."

One of the most significant moments of growth in the life of Thérèse was to come much later. She had been anxious for several months because of a saying she had heard earlier in a sermon, "No one knows whether one is worthy of love or hate." She could hardly have expected much help from the Franciscan preacher who came, with a reputation for "fire and brimstone" sermons, to give a community retreat. In fact, the prioress had warned the Sisters not to consult him as he did not seem to understand the Carmelite way of life! Thérèse was also concerned that he might awaken her over-sensitive nature again. She felt powerless.

However, all her fears were ill founded. After the retreat, she said that she was truly understood: "My soul was like a book which Father [the priest] read better than I.... He launched me full sail on waves of confidence and love which drew me so strongly; but on which I did not dare advance.... He told me that my shortcomings did not cause God any sorrow and, in his place and on his behalf, he told me that God was very pleased with me." She was now able to throw herself into the arms of Jesus with total confidence and trust. She did not have the courage to do it herself; she was powerless. But God did it with the most unlikely instrument of his love!

The Little Way

Thérèse insisted that God was able "to make her grow up in an instant." She said, "The work I had been unable to do in ten years was done by Jesus in an instant." She prayed to God: "For you, time is nothing: a single day is like a thousand years. In an instant you can prepare me to appear before you." At first sight, the turning-points in the life of

Thérèse may appear sudden and dramatic, like Paul's experience on the road to Damascus (Acts 9:1–9). But a deep conversion and change is rarely an isolated moment; it is generally the end-point of a long process. It gathers momentum slowly, gradually, imperceptibly beneath the surface, like an avalanche before it finally breaks on the surface with a landslide. We do not know how long Paul was kicking against the goad before he fell from his horse and was finally touched by God's grace.

Behind the sudden changes in the life of Thérèse there were long periods of waiting, patiently waiting on God's action: "He grants his light only by degrees; so I was careful not to advance his hour and waited patiently till it pleased Jesus to have this hour come." She was to say on her deathbed: "I think that as far as my death is concerned I'll have to have the same patience regarding it as I had to have in the other great events of my life.... I'm really abandoned; I shall wait as long as he wills...how little it takes to lose one's patience." These are some of her last words: "You must not lose patience," she said, "look at how patient I am. You will have to act like this."

Thérèse's discovery of her own weakness and constant need of God's mercy can help us all. We must learn to live with failure and the burden of our own brokenness. It's the way of hope for wounded humanity. She provides a whole spirituality based on acceptance of weakness and renewed conversion. She calls it "The Little Way." It is specially designed for the weak and fragile like herself, the vulnerable, the poor in spirit, for all who wish to become like little children.

Thérèse explained how her way to God grew out of the experience of her own weakness. It is a "little" way—"very short and totally new." It was her own discovery. It is not like many another narrow and rigid approach to God. Here she broke the mold: "I'm too small to climb the steep stair of God." But she discovered that the arms of Jesus could raise her to heaven, like a mother's arms.

Thérèse had a special love for the Shepherd psalm: "My entire soul experienced it," she admitted. But she knew not only the Shepherd psalm (23), but also the Shepherd's heart. The words of Isaiah had revealed it to her when she first discovered them in her search for the Little Way: "He will feed his flock like a shepherd, he will gather the lambs in his arms, he will carry them in his bosom and gently lead those who are with young" (Isaiah 40:11). We are hardly surprised then when she says: "The elevator that must lift me to heaven is your arms, O Jesus! For that, I do not need to grow up; on the contrary, I must remain little, and become ever more so." She had only to be herself— weak, fragile and a little child, to let herself be carried. It is a child's absolute trust.

It took Thérèse a lifetime to achieve this total surrender. She had already spent three and a half years in Carmel, but she still agonized over her "faults," and worried about constantly offending

God. At first, it is true, we can detect in her an element of attempting to earn God's love by her own fidelity. But gradually she discovered that everything is a grace, a free gift: "Jesus has no need of our works, but only of our love."

We are fortunate to have many photographs of Thérèse. One of her best-known commentators, Conrad de Meester, describes through the image of her hand how her confidence gradually developed:

> At first the hand was seeking to grasp, the fingers were clenched and the palms turned downward.... Later the palms turned upward.... The hand was then open, offering, ready to give and in return ready to receive much. It took almost a whole lifetime for this to happen. It was not done with a flick of the wrist.

With Empty Hands

Jesus offers the gift of his kingdom with a reminder that "Whoever does not receive the kingdom of God like a child shall not enter it." To "enter" this kingdom—paradoxically!—we have to "receive" it, as Thérèse did, with open hands: "In the evening of life, I shall stand before you with empty hands." But this kingdom is not something fixed and static. It is something dynamic, powerful, alive, and active. It is God's response to a child's surrender and trust. It is where God rules and reigns when we let him enter, as Thérèse did, to take possession of our lives.

"I read your pages with their burning love for Jesus," her sister told Thérèse after reading part of her life story. "May I tell you? I will: you are possessed by God, literally possessed... I wish I could be possessed by Jesus as you are." In Thérèse, God reigned. Paul knew, too, what this means: "I am still running," he said, "trying to capture the prize for which Christ Jesus captured me" (Philippians 3:14). Thérèse was also captured by love. She says it all in a few lines of her prayer: "I know that you will grant me my desires; I know, too, O my God, that the more you want to give, the more you increase desire. In my heart I feel immense desires; and so I ask you, confidently, to come and take possession of my soul." Her prayer was fully answered.

The Cost of Surrender

We discover the cost of total surrender to love for Thérèse in the great and final testing of her faith. She had written to a priest friend that her "way is all trust and love." But shortly afterward, she wrote again about the "thickest darkness" which had invaded her soul fourteen months earlier. It was Easter and she had coughed up blood just a few days earlier. This was the first summons, a "distant murmur," she called it, "which announced the Bridegroom's arrival." It is risky to assume we can understand just what she experienced at this time. She herself found it almost impossible to explain: "One would have to travel through this dark tunnel to understand its darkness." She was covered in "thick fog" and then suddenly the fog became "more dense." She could not discern any trace of heaven. Everything had disappeared. Her torment redoubled. The darkness borrowed the voice of hellish tormentors and said to her, mockingly, that death would not give her what she hoped for but only "the night of nonexistence.... I do not want to write any longer about it," she added, "I fear I might blaspheme." Even her own little way seemed lost.

She tells us that she was tempted by "the reasoning of the worst materialists...that science will explain everything naturally." Her words at this time have an incredible ring of truth. A few days before she died, her sister Pauline was sitting by her bed. Thérèse pointed outside at a row of chestnut trees and said: "Look! Do you see the black hole...where we can see nothing; it's in a similar hole that I am as far as body and soul are concerned...what darkness! But I am at peace." Near the end, she confided that "the pain was enough to make her lose her reason." She asked her sister not to leave any poisonous medicines around her. She said in a "strangled" voice that she was surprised that there were not more suicides among atheists. But still she tried to smile and appeared "calm." "If I had no faith," she said, "I would have inflicted death on myself without a moment's hesitation...I have made more acts of faith in this last year than all through my whole life." But then she added: "Yet will I trust him."

She said that it might appear from the poems which she wrote during these trials that the veil of faith was almost torn aside for her. But the reality was quite different. "It is no longer a veil for me," she said, "it is a wall that reaches right up to the heavens.... When I sing of the happiness of heaven and of the eternal possession of God, I feel no joy in this, for I sing simply of what I want to believe." She drew her strength repeatedly from the words of Job: "If he should kill me, yet will I trust him" (13:15). Thérèse questioned. She doubted; specifically she doubted heaven: "I don't believe in eternal life. I think that after life there will be nothing more. Everything has vanished for me." But she added, and this is what matters: "All I have is love."

For Thérèse, to follow Jesus is like falling in love. Everything else must fade away. She prayed: "I beg you: release the waters of infinite tenderness pent up within you; and let them well up within my soul." She was determined to remove every obstacle that impeded this torrent of love from invading her soul. She opened to accept it, with all the sacrifices it demanded. She wanted to love "with no other occupation but to pick flowers, flowers of love and sacrifice to offer them to God for his pleasure."

Today we may not choose to speak, like Thérèse, of love's demands as "picking flowers." But the sacrifices that surrender to love's demands are radical, no matter how we speak of them. Nobody knew this better than she did: "To love is to give oneself, to give everything. I do not give in order to receive. It is God whom I love, not myself."

Thérèse is like the Bride in the Song of Songs: "Having given all my wealth for the sake of love," she said, "I reckon that I have given nothing."

≫

Reflections

Wisdom Is Always Young

Read Matthew 18:11–14

Ponder these words:

The new people are young. They understand new things. Childhood is for us the age which knows nothing of old age, that in which one is always striving to learn. Let us always be young, always fresh, always new. Let our whole life be a springtime. Let the fruit that is within us be without old age. Wisdom is always young.

(Clement of Alexandria)

The God of Our Weakness

Read 2 Corinthians 12:7–10

Pause for a moment. Stop what you are doing, and let yourself relax. Let all the tension flow out of your body, all your troubled thoughts fade away. Breathe slowly, and deeply. Be still.... Turn to Jesus. Here I am, Lord, I want you to take me as I am—with all my weaknesses! Jesus, come to me. Help me to make the journey without fear, as Thérèse did, into my heart. Give me the courage to face myself as she did, honestly, and to wait in patience for your coming.

God speaks in silence. Stay in the silence.

A Treasure in Earthen Vessels

Read 2 Corinthians 4:7–11

God will shed his light into the darkness of your mind and heart—the hidden depths of your fears, anxieties, and guilt. He will speak to you in the silence. Be patient. Nothing is happening. Just persevere. He will look upon his weak and lonely creature and help you to accept yourself and all your human limitations. God is God; let him be God in you. He will set you free. Your weakness is no obstacle to intimacy with him. Listen to the words of Thérèse: "I feel that if you found a soul weaker and littler than mine, you would be pleased to grant it still greater favors, provided it abandoned itself with total confidence to your infinite mercy."

Prayer

Abandonment Is the Sweet Fruit of Love
No, nothing worries me.
Nothing can trouble me.
My soul knows how to fly
Higher than the lark.
Above the clouds
The sky is always blue.
One touches the shores
Where God reigns.

5

The Burning Heart

"HAD I BEEN A PRIEST I would have studied Hebrew and Greek in depth," Thérèse once said, "in order to know God's mind as he deigned to express it in our human language." She longed to read the Scriptures in the original. We know that the many different translations "distressed" her. She wanted to know the exact meaning of the biblical terms. The Jesus she discovered in the Gospels was "full of grace and truth." But what do the terms "grace" and "truth" mean? Thérèse herself may not have known precisely, but her teaching on the heart of Jesus gives a profound insight into their meaning. Both terms belong to the vocabulary of the covenant.

God's Enduring Love

The Hebrew word for grace is "hesed." It refers to God's merciful love and describes a relationship between God and his people when he chose them as his own possession and promised to lead them out of slavery into the Promised Land: "It was for love of you and to keep the oath he swore to your fathers that Yahweh brought you out with a mighty hand and redeemed you from the house of slavery" (Deuteronomy 7:8).

There is no "hesed" on the basis of legal justice. It is mercy through and through; it is the free gift of God's love. It is commonly linked with the Hebrew word "emeth," which means "truth" in the sense of God's "fidelity" to his own love in spite of his people's sins and failures: "Indeed, how good is the Lord, eternal his merciful love. He is faithful from age to age" (Psalm 99:5). "Hesed" is God's enduring love for a wayward people. Paul's words express the meaning well: "We may be unfaithful, but he is always faithful, for he cannot disown his own self" (2 Timothy 2:13). God is always true to his love.

But "hesed" is not something vague or nebulous. It is a real, flesh and blood term. It is closely linked with another Old Testament word for merciful love, "rahamim," which denotes a mother's love for the child of her womb. The psalmist himself cries out at the marvels of this love: "For it was you who created my being, knit me together in my mother's womb" (Psalm 139:13). This love, too, is enduring and freely given, but it has all the additional feminine qualities of a mother's tender love. It is patient and understanding and always ready to forgive. This was the kind of love Thérèse discovered in the heart of God when she searched the Scriptures for confirmation of her "Little Way."

We might expect that Thérèse searched the Gospels first, but she didn't. She first explored the Old Testament. She found these words of wisdom in the book of Proverbs: "Whoever is a little one, let him come to me" (9:4). She was still unsatisfied. She wanted to know what God would do for the little ones. "I continued my search," she said, and she found the words of Isaiah: "As one whom a mother caresses so will I comfort you...you will be carried at the breast" (66:13). She could have found the same kind of love again in other words of Isaiah: "Can a woman forget her babe at the breast, feel no pity for the child of her womb? Even if she were to forget, I shall not forget you" (49:15).

Thérèse discovered the feminine in the heart of God. "I have always felt at the bottom of my heart that God is more tender than any mother," she said. She expressed it beautifully in one of her poems:

> O you who knew how to create the mother's heart,
> I find in you the tenderest of Fathers!
> My only Love, Jesus, Eternal Word,
> For me your heart is more than maternal.

The New Heart

Thérèse calls for surrender in total confidence and trust. The foundation of her teaching is this tender and enduring love in the heart of God, our Mother. God is constantly reminding his people of it: "I will betroth you to myself forever, betroth you with integrity and justice, with tenderness and love; I will betroth you to myself with faithfulness" (Hosea 2:19). The covenant was a constant reminder to his people of God's merciful love which "led them with the cords of compassion, with the bands of love" (Hosea 11:4). But the prophets also spoke of a future covenant. Jeremiah had foretold it: "I will put my law within them, and I will write it upon their hearts.... I will forgive their iniquity, and I will remember their sins no more" (Jeremiah 31:33). Ezekiel takes up these words and develops them further: "A new heart I will give you, and a new spirit I will put within you; and I will take out of your flesh the heart of stone and give you a heart of flesh" (Ezekiel 36:26).

Thérèse discovers this "new heart" in the heart of Jesus. He alone is "full of grace and truth." Paul tells us that "in him all the promises of God find their Yes" (2 Corinthians 1:20). He is the fulfillment—God's last word on merciful love! He is the "new heart," the new covenant, God's enduring love for his people in the flesh. Thérèse invites everyone to surrender to this merciful love. She asked God for a "legion" of others like herself, who would be worthy of his love. She herself had given the example:

> O Heart of Jesus, treasure of tenderness,
> You yourself are my happiness, my only hope.

Pictures of the Sacred Heart were numerous in Thérèse's day; she had even sketched one herself. Her spiritual director, Father Pichon, often referred to the Sacred Heart in his letters. She had heard sermons about it; she had been solemnly consecrated to the Sacred Heart in the basilica of Montmartre, but Thérèse herself seldom spoke of it. She used the expression "Sacred Heart" only once in her autobiography. She addressed only one of her twenty-one prayers to the Sacred Heart. The few of her poems that refer to it directly were composed at the request of her godmother, Sister Marie of the Sacred Heart.

Thérèse was not entirely at ease with the representations of the heart of Jesus common in her day, just as some people today may not feel at ease with them. She would confide in her sister Celine, after she had accompanied her other sister Leonie to Paray-le-Monial for the second centenary of the death of St. Margaret Mary: "You know, I don't see the Sacred Heart as others do! I think that the heart of my Spouse is mine alone, just as mine is his alone, and I speak to him then in the solitude of this delightful heart-to-heart exchange, waiting for the day when I will contemplate him face to face." We can see more clearly the originality of her approach by considering some of the details in the traditional representations of the Sacred Heart that did in fact appeal to Thérèse.

Thérèse was given a picture of the heart of Mary when she was fourteen years old. It was to mark her reception as a child of Mary. Some of its details are quite significant. The flaming heart is pierced with a lance and two small doves nestle in it, while a third is still in flight on its way to entering it. Underneath the heart is a castle or fortress firmly built on a rock. At the bottom of the picture we read the words: "Heart of Mary, you are the only fortress from which the enemy cannot expel me." In the heart of Mary, Thérèse felt safe and at rest. It was for her a place of refuge into which she could enter to lose and hide herself. She had already begun to paint small pictures at the age of eleven. But this picture was to influence her considerably when she later painted her own picture of the heart of Jesus a few months after she entered Carmel.

In this later picture, we see a traditional representation of the heart of Jesus. It burns with the fire of love. A crown of thorns encircles it and a cross emerges from the flames. Drops of blood trickle down from it—as Thérèse had seen years earlier in another picture—and she was consumed with a thirst to gather them to save souls: "I was struck by the blood flowing from one of the divine hands... I was resolved to remain in spirit at the foot of the cross." The verse on this picture affirms again the redemptive value of sacrifice: "What a joy it is to suffer with Jesus and for Jesus!" This is a variation of the theme written by Thérèse herself on the first card she ever received when she was eleven years old: "Suffering passes; to have suffered well remains forever."

But the heart in this picture also illustrates another favorite theme of Thérèse. It is poised above a little boat that is sailing toward it on a wide-open sea. When she was only six or seven years old, Thérèse caught her first glimpse of the sea. She was thrilled with "its majesty and the roaring of its waves." "Everything about it spoke to my soul," she said, "of God's grandeur and power." His strong heart stirred for her in the pounding of its waves. In the evening, she sat with her sister Pauline and watched the setting sun shedding a trail of light to guide the path of a little white-sailed vessel. Thérèse realized that the heavenly body which allowed the boat to sail in total security was the heart of Jesus. So his heart became her magnet: "I made the resolution," she said, "never to wander far from the glance of Jesus in order to travel peacefully toward the eternal shore."

In her moments of darkness, the sailboat also had a special significance. While she was still quite young, her sister Celine gave her a little boat with the word "abandonment" engraved on the hull to encourage her. On the sail was inscribed a verse from the Song of Songs: "I sleep but my heart keeps vigil" (5:2). It was to remain a constant reminder for Thérèse. Even if Jesus seemed to be asleep and doing nothing in the storm, his heart still watched over her with loving care: "The most absolute aridity and almost total abandonment were my lot," she said on one occasion. "Jesus was sleeping as usual in my boat; ah! I see very well how rarely souls allow him to sleep peacefully within them." She was to express it all in a few lines of one of her poems:

Living on Love, when Jesus is sleeping,
Is rest on stormy seas.
Oh! don't fear that I'll wake you.
I'm waiting in peace for heaven's shore...
Rest in Safety.

In this same picture of Thérèse there is also a dove resting on a rock which overlooks the sea. The detail recalls one of the old-style representations of the Sacred Heart which Thérèse found more acceptable. In it the heart is presented as the "hollow of the rock." Thérèse wanted to lose, hide herself, and rest in the heart of Jesus just as she did in the heart of Mary. It was her place of refuge and repose. She often meditated on the Song of Songs where the Bridegroom invites his beloved—his dove—to come and curl up against him: "Come then, my love, my lovely one, come. My dove, hiding in the cleft of the rock, in the coverts of the cliff" (2:14).

The heart of Jesus was the place where Thérèse could enter and rest in the safety of his love. She was never deterred by her own helplessness. For her, the word "mercy" took on the full literal meaning of misericordia, that is, "to give misery a place in the heart." It is not the image of the condescending father patting his little child benignly on the head. Jesus takes Thérèse with all her misery into his own heart and places her there. The words of the psalm were surely not lost on Thérèse: "From the dust he lifts up the lowly, from his misery he raises the poor" (113:7). Again and again she spoke of her hiding-place in his heart: "I want to hide myself in you, O Jesus! Lovers must have solitude; a heart-to-heart lasting day and night." Her sister Pauline wrote a few words on one of Thérèse's paintings: "Love me and do not fear me...every time you raise your heart to me by love I receive it in my hands and then it is in safety." The lesson was not lost on Thérèse. She herself returned constantly to the same theme: "It is to you alone, Jesus, that I'm attached; it's into your arms that I run and hide... I make my home in your hearth. It's in your ever-infinite goodness that I want to lose myself...rest and hide myself...O heart of Jesus."

The image of the "dove" is closely linked with the image of the face in the Song of Songs:

> Show me your face,
> let me hear your voice;
> for your voice is sweet
> and your face is beautiful (2:14).

So, too, is the image of the heart of Jesus and his face for Thérèse: "To sleep on his heart so close to his face, such is my heaven." However, it is not just a question of intimacy. It is complete oneness: "I beg you to see me when you look upon the face of Jesus," she prayed, "see me in his heart burning with love."

Here again we see the originality of Thérèse. The devotion to the face of Jesus that she had known since childhood stressed the idea of reparation. The face was commonly depicted as blood-stained and profaned by abuses. Thérèse was never to deny this aspect in her devotion: "Even in my heart," she would say, "the blasphemy resounds." She was also quite explicit in her prayer: "I want to work for your love alone. All I want is to please you and to console your Sacred Heart."

But for Thérèse it was not the blasphemies that made the face of Jesus writhe in pain. It was his love that drove him to his passion and death. She especially liked one representation of her own day which linked the Sacred Heart and the face of Jesus. On the back of it she could read the words: "If the heart of Jesus is the symbol of love, his adorable face is its eloquent expression." For Thérèse, devotion to the face of Jesus and his heart was essentially one. It was the contemplation of his love:

> Your face is my only homeland.
> It's my kingdom of love.

It is hardly surprising that Thérèse felt specially drawn to the Gospel of John. For her profession, her sister gave her a picture of the beloved disciple resting on the breast of Jesus, which she liked very much. Above the two figures was a caption, "The Life of Union," with a few words of explanation: "Whoever loves me will be loved by my Father and we will be in him." It was an illustration for Thérèse of a Gospel saying dear to her heart: "Those who love me will be loved by my Father and we will come to him and make our home with him" (John 14:23). Underneath the figures are the words: "Just as fire easily enflames what is dry, so your soul will be entirely filled by me, and I myself will be in you."

We can surmise how deeply Thérèse had pondered the mystery of the indwelling presence of the Trinity in the heart of the believer. We see the image of the Father and the Spirit as a dove within a circle around the heads of Jesus and John in this picture. It expresses one of Thérèse's great desires: to rest against the heart of Jesus like the beloved disciple, and to allow her Beloved to find in her "the place of his rest." But she knew that to rest on the breast of Jesus like St. John and to enter into his heart was to open herself also to the Father and the Son. She said it all in a few lines:

> On the evening of love, speaking without parable,
> Jesus said: "If anyone wishes to love me
> All his life, let him keep my word.
> My Father and I will come to visit him.
> And we will make his heart our dwelling.

But there was one other picture which appealed to Thérèse more than all others. To explore the insights revealed in it is to penetrate right to the core of John's Gospel. It is entitled, "The Heart of Christ in the Bosom of the Trinity." Again, the Father and the Spirit are represented by way of background to the figure of Jesus, who receives the fullness of the Spirit from the Father to communicate it in turn to others. It is the scene of the baptism in John: "The man on whom you see the Spirit come down and rest is the one who is to baptize with the Holy Spirit" (John 1:33). Mary and Joseph are also in the picture inviting a pilgrim with staff to come to the heart of Jesus. Jesus stands at the center of the picture, the great Mediator uniting in his heart both heaven and earth. With his finger, he points to his heart and invites every pilgrim to enter through it into the depths of the Trinity.

In the Gospel of John, Jesus also points to his own heart as the source of the Spirit: "Out of his heart shall flow torrents of living water.... Now this he said about the Spirit which those who believed in him were to receive" (7:38–39).

Thérèse recalls the words of Jesus: "He who is thirsty let him come to me and drink" (John 7:37). Like the thirsty deer, she says, "we long for this water." In the heart of the Samaritan woman, one of Thérèse's favorite Gospel characters, this living water was like a spring "welling up into eternal life" (John 4:14). The evangelist directs us forward to the glorifying death and resurrection of Jesus for the final outpouring of this Spirit: "The Spirit had not yet been given because Jesus had not yet been glorified." It was to this supreme moment in his life that Jesus also directed his disciples when he said: "And I, if I be lifted up, will draw everyone to myself" (John 12:32). He finally bowed his head on the cross and—literally—"handed over the Spirit." One of the soldiers opened his side with a lance and the waters of the Spirit flowed from his pierced heart: "at once there came forth blood and water"

(John 19:34). The risen Jesus "breathes" on his disciples as he points to his wounded side and says: "receive the Holy Spirit" (John 20:22).

Thérèse longed to drink from these waters of the Spirit flowing from the heart of Jesus: "O my Jesus! I thirst for this water," she said, "I crave for it." It is all there in a few lines of her poem:

> As a stag in its ardent thirst
> longs for running springs,
> O Jesus! I run, faltering, to you.

Thérèse invites everyone to the heart of Jesus to drink with her from the waters of the Spirit: "The Spirit of love sets me aflame with his fire," she said. "Flame of love consume me unceasingly...I want to be set on fire with his love."

Reflections

Hide Not Your Face, Lord

Read the Song of Songs 2:10–14

Jesus invites us to hide and lose ourselves, like Thérèse, in his heart. Take all your human limitations with you as you listen to his words, "Come to me...you will find rest...I will give you rest. I am meek and humble of heart."

I want to be set on fire with your love, Lord. I know that weakness is no obstacle. It's a stepping-stone. I have only to throw myself into your arms with confidence and accept the gift of your love. Thérèse encourages me. I pray with her words: "I beg you to release the waters of infinite tenderness pent up within you; and let them well up within my soul.... I want to work for your love alone. All I want is to please you and to console your Sacred Heart...you are happy not to hold back the waves of infinite tenderness within you." Help me, Lord, to remove the obstacles to your love. Let your love penetrate me and surround me. Help me, Lord, to persevere in prayer; hide not your face from me, for in you have I put my trust. If in the darkness you still hide from me, the words of Thérèse will give me consolation:

> If I cannot see the brilliance of your Face
> or hear your sweet voice,
> O my God, I can live by your grace,
> I can rest on your Sacred Heart.

God Is Always Faithful

Read Deuteronomy 7:6–9

Reflect for a few moments. I have been chosen by God as his own possession out of so many others more worthy of his love. It was not for any gifts or talents of mine that God chose me. It is because he loves me and is faithful to his promises. Thérèse opened the Gospels at random and discovered her vocation as she read these words: "Going up into the mountains he called to himself those he want-ed' (Mark 3:13). I find this lesson again on the lips of Jesus: "You did not choose me, no, I chose you" (John 15:16). Here lies the mystery of my calling too, my life-story. The pattern of God's love never changes: he chooses what is foolish in the world to shame the wise; what is weak to shame the strong.

Pause. Reflect quietly. Open your heart to his love. Persevere in prayer.

Prayer

How I Want to Love You

Divine Jesus, listen to my prayer.
By my love I want to make you rejoice.
You know well, I want to please you alone.
Deign to grant my most ardent desire.
I accept the trials of this sad exile
To delight you and to console your heart.
But change all my works into love,
O my Spouse, my Beloved Savior.

6

Prayer

IN THE PLAY SHADOWLANDS there is a scene which illustrates much of what Thérèse has to tell us about prayer. C. S. Lewis is talking with his agnostic friend. He says, "Prayer? I pray all the time these days. If I stopped praying, I think I'd stop living."

"And God hears your prayer, doesn't he?' his friend chides him in reply. "I hear your wife's getting better."

"Yes, she is," Lewis replies, "but that's not why I pray. I pray because the need flows out of me all the time, waking and sleeping. It doesn't change God. It changes me."

"Now that I understand," his friend replies. "That's the first sensible thing I've heard anyone say on the subject."

He would have heard a lot deeper, more original, and even more sensible things had he read what Thérèse has to say on the subject.

A Surge of the Heart

"For me, prayer is an aspiration of the heart." Thérèse distills the essence of prayer into this one short phrase. It gives her pride of place today with the great doctors of the Church in the new Catechism's splendid treatment of prayer. So much for the value and the relevance of her teaching. Prayer is a fling of the heart to the heart of God, an outburst of love. To pray with Thérèse is to let the heart reach out to God with longings, like the heart of the psalmist: "O God, you are my God, for you I long; for you my soul is thirsting. My body pines for you like a dry, weary land without water" (Psalm 63:1). It's the cry of an exiled heart.

Thérèse loved to pray with the Gospels. There she discovered the heart of prayer: "Lord, that I may see.... Lord, be merciful to me a sinner.... Save us, Lord, we perish.... I believe, Lord, help my unbelief. Jesus, Son of David, have pity on me.... I thirst.... Lord, to whom should we go?... My Lord and my God...." The list is endless. These prayers are like arrows piercing straight to the heart of God. Thérèse knew them well and made them her own.

But she was not afraid to coin her own also. She had her favorites. They were born of her own needs, experiences, and intimate conversations with Jesus. We find these scattered throughout her writings. They break upon us when we least expect them and express the deepest longings of her heart: "O Jesus, my love... Jesus is my only love... Jesus, make me resemble you. Draw me...." Again, the list is endless. Her prayer of offering to Merciful Love is like a litany of aspirations: "I long to love you...

come, and take possession of my soul... stay close to me... I want to console you. I want to work for your love alone...give yourself to me forever...continue to consume me, Lord." They are all part of her hunger and thirst for God, her endless, aching need. She may not have heard of the medieval mystical book, *The Cloud of Unknowing,* but her teaching is one with it: "Beat upon that thick cloud of unknowing with a sharp dart of longing love." Her aspirations, too, are flames of love.

Thérèse exclaimed, "It is not necessary to read from a book some beautiful formulae composed for the occasion." She tells us that these prayers only gave her a headache: "I say very simply to God what I want to say, without composing beautiful sentences, and he always understands me...complicated prayers are all very well, but they are not for simple souls like me." Thérèse was not locked into any method or rigid form of prayer. Her approach to God was the way of a child, simple and direct. She never referred to degrees or stages of prayer.

"I love very much these prayers in common with others," she said. The psalms had a special place in her heart. The Gospels supported her love for community prayer: "Where two or three are gathered together in my name, there am I in the midst of them." She did not minimize in any way the value of vocal prayer. The dry words took on deep meaning for her when she pondered them quietly in the light of her own experience. She transformed them by the power of her love. She admitted that her mind was often empty and distracted. At times not a single thought came to her about God: "At these times," she said, "I recite the Our Father very slowly, and then the Angelus. These prayers give me great joy." But she warned: "We must never recite them in a hurry." Her teaching is Gospel teaching: "Do not heap up empty phrases as the gentiles do."

A Thinking Heart

The Lord's Prayer led Thérèse into deep prayer. Her sister Celine found her alone one day in her convent room. Her eyes were brimming. "Why the tears?" Celine asked.

Thérèse replied: "I was just thinking what a wonderful thing it is to be able to call God our Father." Her heart had already gone out to him. What an aspiration of love! Thérèse knew that she did not have to ponder every word or every phrase every time. There is a pain hidden in the exile's heart—a hunger, a thirst, a longing, a desire for the homeland. The Our Father became a kind of springboard for her to set free the wings of prayer—to reach out in love.

Thérèse was at ease with many ways of praying. She practiced prayerful reflection, even from an early age. But she did not practice it in the way the books tell us to. Often it was meditation, unawares. She recalled a fishing expedition with her father. There she sat on the green river bank: "I knew nothing of meditation," she said later, "but my thoughts ran deep...earth seemed a land of exile and I dreamt of heaven." Her pilgrim soul in exile was longing for home. This was prayer. It was the sigh of an ever watchful, heaven-directed heart. It was an aspiration.

Thérèse was to confess later that her school days were the five saddest years of her life. But she recalled how on one occasion she lay awake, "alone, with my thoughts sunk in deep prayer." She used to spend some time in hiding, "thinking about God, about life, about eternity," she said. Then she reflected: "I was practicing mental prayer without realizing it. God was teaching me in some secret way."

The beauty of the world around her stirred Thérèse deeply, like her first glimpse of the sea: "Never will I forget the impression the sea made upon me; I couldn't take my eyes off it since its majesty, the roaring of its waves, everything spoke to my soul of God's grandeur and power." So, too, her first glimpse of the Alps—"its summits lost in the clouds, its graceful waterfalls, its deep valleys, its steep ravines, the calm waters of a lake." All these left her breathless at a world so charged with the presence of God. She reflected: "When I saw all these beauties, very profound thoughts came to life in my soul. I seemed to understand already the grandeur of God and the marvels of heaven.... I understood how easy it is to become all wrapped up in self.... I shall easily forget my own little interests, recalling the grandeur and the power of God." She resolved never to forget these experiences, even later in Carmel: "I shall remember what I see today," she said, "and that will give me courage."

Thérèse knew moments of great consolation. Her First Communion was full of joy: "Tears of happiness flowed and all the joys of heaven came flooding into a human heart." The second time she received Communion also brought "an indescribable sense of joy." Indeed, at times, her only consolation was to wait before the Blessed Sacrament in silent prayer. But this wasn't always the way. Even after Holy Communion, she was to say later in life, "I don't know of any moment at which I experience less consolation."

She often fell asleep during her time of thanksgiving. It didn't worry her. "Little children are no less pleasing when they are asleep." She once painted a backdrop for the convent chapel. They asked her later about the little "sleeping" angel on it. "That's me," she replied, "asleep at prayer!" Again, she looked to the Gospels for meaning. There she saw Jesus at ease, cushioned, at rest, "asleep in the boat," she said, "and I don't want to waken him."

In fact, Thérèse was to know moments of intense dryness and unrelieved darkness during her prayer. The thought of heaven became nothing but conflict and torment for her: "I can no longer pray," she said on one occasion. She had leaped so often into her Father's arms, but gone now were those arms of love, outstretched caressingly.

Everything was darkness, emptiness, void—no maps, no rudder, no compass. She had long since thrown them away. Jesus was still asleep. She was alone, storm-tossed on a dark and turbulent sea. But still she had no thought for herself. Prayer was "his" time; only "his" comfort mattered. Her confidence was at full reach; it could hardly be stretched further. All she could say, she tells us, is one word: "Jesus." But that word says everything. His joy, not hers, was all that mattered. To give him pleasure. That was her prayer.

At the end of her life, her prayer was constant—simple, deep, spontaneous, and childlike. It was her prayer of complete and absolute trust. But this was God's final gift. Her prayer-life, too, had to develop gradually, with her ever-deepening surrender. It was not always easy. It became a prayer of total surrender in the darkness of faith to the mystery of love. But not without dryness and failures, and indeed not without effort, determination, and perseverance.

An Expanding Heart

For Thérèse, prayer was always a thing of the heart. It was nothing if it was not love: "It is only love that can expand my heart." So she said the same about prayer: "It expands my soul and unites me to Jesus." Mother Teresa of Calcutta was once asked what she thought about prayer. She replied: "Prayer enlarges the heart until it is capable of containing God's gift of himself. Ask and seek, and your heart will grow big enough to receive him and keep him as your own." Teresa of Avila said the same. She described the effect of prayer with the words of a psalm: "You have expanded my heart." John of the Cross echoed this faithfully: "How tenderly you swell my heart with love!"

Thérèse was heir to this rich Carmelite tradition of prayer. There is nothing narrow or cramped about it. It opens wide the human heart and releases its capacity for love. The lesson is there in the Gospels: "If you who are evil know how to give good gifts to your children, how much more will the heavenly Father give the Holy Spirit to those who ask him" (Luke 11:13). The Spirit of love is God's response to every aspiration. Thérèse said the same thing in her own way. Prayer expanded her soul to receive God's gift of his love.

"Lovers must have solitude," Thérèse said, "a heart-to-heart lasting day and night." These few words capture much of what is characteristic in Carmelite prayer. It is an exchange of love; an exchange or dialogue that demands a quiet place for sharing. An isolated moment, a fleeting glance is not enough. Extended time is also needed. Thérèse had seen how in the Gospels Jesus often withdrew to be alone in loving communion with his Father, even spending "the whole night in prayer to God." She had heard the invitation to follow his example: "Go into your room, shut the door, and pray to your Father in secret." She had responded to the demand for persevering prayer: "We ought always to pray and never to lose heart." It was all there for her in the need which lovers have to spend lots of time together, communing with one another.

But Thérèse has still more to tell us about this exchange of love: "The heart of my Beloved is mine alone," she said, "just as mine is his alone." Her prayer called for unconditional surrender, a communion that could finally be consummated only in total self-giving love, like the love of Jesus on Calvary. It was also a joyful gift of self: "I speak to him," she said, "in the solitude of this delightful heart-to-heart." She did this, she said, "while waiting for the day when I will contemplate him face to face." She said of her surrender to Merciful Love that she wanted "to renew it again and again, with every beat of my heart, until the shadows disappear, and I can tell you yet again of my love, forever, face to face." Her communion of love with God in quiet prayer was for her heaven anticipated, experienced already here and now.

When Thérèse prayed she was always in touch with her own weakness. Powerless, she stood at the foot of the stairs helpless to climb, like a little child. This was her own image: God stood at the top, like a mother, and watched her efforts. She made the effort, and the effort had to be made. But she was weak and frail and helpless. God stooped to raise her to himself. She discovered a great truth about prayer: it is not an achievement, it is God's gift—his gift to those who pray. Her prayer did not change God. It changed her, purifying and transforming her into his love. She was surrendering to love: "Now resignation is my only guide," she said, "the only compass I have to steer by."

She calls prayer her "all-powerful weapon...the only strength I have...it's like a queen with easy access to the king. She can obtain whatever she asks for, as Jesus promised: ask...seek...knock." Thérèse discovered this from her own experience: "My prayers are always granted," she said. "He always gives me what I desire, or rather, he has made me desire what he wants to give me." Prayer, she says, is like a mighty crane, with a lever and a support—the fulcrum, where the lever rests and turns. She recalls the words of a Greek philosopher, Archimedes: "Give me a lever and a fulcrum and I will lift the world." We have that mighty crane, she says. It's prayer, her "all-powerful weapon." It can raise the world.

Open to the Spirit

In Masefield's play, *The Trial of Jesus,* the centurion Longinus talks to a Roman matron, Procula, who asks the question: "Do you think he is dead?"

He replies, "No, lady, I don't."

"Then where is he?" she asks.

Longinus replies, "Let loose in the world."

The Spirit of Jesus is alive—here, there, everywhere. Jesus is always present in the Spirit. Thérèse does not often speak about the Spirit of Jesus. But she described in her own original way how he worked within her at prayer and outside prayer:

The Lord has no need of books or teachers to instruct our souls. He, the Teacher of teachers, instructs us without noise of words. I have never heard him speak, yet I know he is within me. He is there, always guiding and inspiring me; and just when I need them most, lights hitherto unseen break in upon me. This is not as a rule during my prayers, but in the midst of my daily duties.

These words are a deep insight into the meaning of Paul's words: "Likewise the Spirit helps us in our weakness; for we do not know how to pray as we ought, but the Spirit himself intercedes for us with sighs too deep for words."

Prayer, for Thérèse, is not just the time spent in church, at Mass, on one's knees. It's being open to the Spirit of Jesus—always. This is how she described his action in her life "here and now." It's her variation of the sacrament of the present moment:

I have frequently noticed that Jesus does not want me to lay up provisions; he nourishes me at each moment with a totally new food; I find it within me without my knowing how it is there. I believe it is Jesus himself hidden in the depths of my poor little heart: he is giving me the grace of acting within me, making me think of all he desires me to do at the present moment.

Thérèse wrote a number of prayers, twenty-one in all. The pearl is her offering to Merciful Love. It is her whole teaching in prayer-form. It contains her act of total surrender two years before her death. This offering had still to be lived out in full during the final darkness of her night of faith. It is a prayer out of the depths, an extended aspiration. Through it we are drawn into what she has called her "heart-to-heart" communion with Jesus, her exchange of love with God in prayer.

But it is possible to take practically any passage of her writings and see how the spirit of prayer pervades everything. Her words were not written for worldwide readers; rather, they were the intimate outpourings of her soul under the action of the Spirit: "Without showing himself, without making his voice heard, Jesus teaches me in secret. It is not by means of books." The words of Thérèse should be read, like the Gospels, in the same spirit in which they were written: prayerfully. Her writings, like the Gospels, give us beautiful prayers and aspirations. They also contain inspiring teaching on prayer, but like the Gospels, too, her writings are prayer. She is like the evangelist in the early Church community. She is, like him, open at all times to the Spirit. The writings of Thérèse, like the Gospels, have to be pondered deeply, lovingly, and constantly, and with an open heart ever ready to receive the gift of prayer. She is not just concerned to teach us about prayer, or to give us prayers. She invites us to share her spirit of prayer. That spirit—ultimately—is not taught, it's caught.

For Thérèse, to pray is to be one with the missionary outreach of the Church. She burned with an ardent desire to be a missionary: "I would want to preach the Gospel on all the five continents simultaneously and even to the most remote isles. I would be a missionary, not for a few years only but until the consummation of the ages." We have a photograph of Thérèse holding a parchment with the words of Teresa of Avila written on it: "I would give a thousand lives to save one soul." She had her spiritual brothers, missionaries who traveled as she herself longed "to spread on heathen soil the glorious standard of the cross." She supported them with her prayers. "The zeal of a Carmelite," she tells us, "embraces the whole world." She wanted to go to the missions herself, but bad health prevented her. Still, she shares the title of principal patron of the missions with Francis Xavier, although she never left her cloister. Such was the missionary value of her prayer. Her life is a living commentary on the words of the Gospel: "Pray the Lord of the harvest..."

Thérèse found her vocation at the heart of the Church: it was love. "I understood that it was love alone that made the Church's members act." To pray in her way is to love and so to be one with all the needs of the Church. Thérèse did not feel it necessary to specify the object of her prayers, to mention this or that intention. She compared her prayer to a torrent which drags everything with it when it crashes into the sea of God's love. Her prayer carried with it all those to whom she was united in love, their needs, and their intentions—indeed, the Church with all its needs. She reflected on some words from the Song of Songs and explained how this is possible: "Draw me, we shall run after you in the odor of your ointments. This simple statement, 'Draw me,' suffices; I understand, Lord, that when a soul allows herself to be captivated by the odor of your ointments, she cannot run alone, all the souls whom she loves follow in her train." Such, then, was her witness to the power of prayer to answer all the needs of the people of God.

All things are possible through the power of prayer. There is only one condition. The lesson of Thérèse is as old as the Desert Fathers:

> Abba Lot went to see Abba Joseph and said: "Abba, as much as I am able, I practice my little rule, keep all my little fasts, say my prayers, keep the silence, and keep my thoughts clean. What else should I do? Then the old man stood up and stretched out his hands toward heaven, and his fingers became like ten torches of flame. And he said: "Why not be turned into fire?"

Why not be turned into fire? It is possible: "I have found the secret of possessing your flame," Thérèse cried out to God. "It is necessary that it

lower itself to nothingness and transform this nothingness into fire."

Reflections

Reach out to Jesus

Read Psalms 42 (41)–43 (42); 63 (62); 84 (83)

Pause. Ask yourself the question: How do I
feel right now, at this moment? Answer honestly.

Let your heart reach out to Jesus; look at him.
Make up your own aspiration to suit your feeling at
this moment, here and now. It shouldn't be longer
than five words. The shorter the better!

Focus on Jesus. Repeat your aspiration
again...again...again.

The aspiration will begin to peter out, but the
effect remains. Rest in the silence for five minutes...ten...fifteen... Stay there just loving, in the
silence. If everything dries up, repeat the aspiration...one word. Let yourself be loved. Let yourself
be changed into love. Just stay in the silence.

Speak Simply to God

Read Matthew 6:7–8

Consider this passage from Thérèse:

I say very simply to God what I wish to
say, without composing beautiful sentences, and he always understands me.

Don't analyze it too much, just let it speak to you. Read it with your heart, with an open mind. Try to catch the spirit. Let it seep in, deeper and deeper, shaping your heart to the heart of Thérèse. Go with the movement...the flow...her mood...her feelings...the whole spirit of the passage. Let Thérèse draw you. Surrender to the Spirit speaking through her, instructing...guiding...inspiring...nourishing...

You Just Can't Pray

Read Matthew 6:9–13; Luke 11:2–4

Sometimes when my mind is in such great dryness that it is impossible to draw forth one single thought to unite me with God, I recite very slowly an "Our Father" and then the angelic salutation; then these prayers give me great delight; they nourish my soul much more than if I had recited them in haste a hundred times.

Now try to do what Thérèse did, reciting the Our Father (or the Angelus, or a Hail Mary, or the Magnificat). There's no hurry, no rush. Concentrate on an easy rhythm, a lingering pace. Just say one Our Father, slowly, calmly, quietly. Ponder the words...one phrase, one word: Father...heaven...kingdom... Stay with the prayer. God is nourishing you.

Take a stroll in the country or a walk in the park, not with any ulterior motive but just to relax. Enjoy yourself. Just be. We think too much...

reflecting...analyzing...philosophizing...judging.
We talk too much...words...words...words...
noise...noise...noise. Be still...aware...alive. Listen to
nature, the harmony. Be aware of the movements
around you. Just look—a cloud, a star, a flower, a
fading leaf, a bird, a stone. Look. Listen. Smell.
Touch. Taste. Slowly, he will reveal himself, ever
so slowly...

Prayer

Jesus Alone

My burning heart wants to give itself unceas-
  ingly.
It needs to prove its tenderness.
Ah! Who will be able to understand my love?
What heart will want to pay me in return?
But I crave this return in vain.
Jesus, you alone can satisfy my soul.
Nothing can charm me here below.
True happiness cannot be found here
My only peace, my only happiness,
My only love is you, Lord!...

7

Repentance

"REPENT AND BELIEVE the Gospel" (Mark 1:15). These are the words that Jesus addressed to the world before he called his first disciples. The word "repent" has a special meaning in the Gospels. It is not a summons to mortification, penance, or self-denial as such. These have a place—and an important place for those who are called to take up the cross daily and follow Jesus. This call of Jesus to "repent" has nothing to do with the extraordinary penances we so often read about in the lives of some of the saints. Thérèse even warns us against these. They had no place in her approach to God: "I had no attraction for these kinds of mortifications," she tells us. "My mortifications consisted in breaking my will, always so ready to impose itself on others, holding back a reply, rendering little services without any recognition...my penances consisted in mortifying my self-love. This did me much more good than any corporal penances." During her final illness, her superior insisted that she warm her "alpargates"—the cord sandals worn in Carmel at the time. Thérèse commented: "Others will go to heaven with their instruments of penance, but I will go with a heater!" Then she adds: "However, it is love and obedience alone that count."

Homecoming

"Penance" in the Gospel sense means a change of mind and heart. When Luke wants to describe the impact of the first Christians on the world around them, he uses a word "ana-histēmi" meaning "to stand on its head" (Acts 17:6). His sentence can only be translated, literally, "they turned the world upside down." The challenge of the early Christians was a total reversal of commonly accepted values. Jesus calls for a whole new mindset: Gospel values. For Paul, it means putting on the mind of Christ: "Let this mind be in you which was also in Christ Jesus...he emptied himself...humbled himself and became obedient unto death..." (Philippians 2:5, 8).

But behind the word "penance" lies another word from the vocabulary of the people of God. It's the word "shubh," meaning "to return." It's used to refer to God's people in exile, when God takes them by the hand and leads them out of slavery and back to the Promised Land. This is the same God who has chosen a people for himself, a nation set apart. Though their sins are like scarlet, Yahweh is always "a God of tenderness and compassion, slow to anger, rich in kindness and faithfulness...forgiving faults, transgression, sin" (Psalm 103:8).

"Repentance" is a kind of homecoming like this, a return to the warmth of God's love. The image of the Prodigal Son captures the idea beautifully in story form. "Yes, I feel it," Thérèse said. "Even though I had on my conscience all the sins that can be committed, I would go, my heart broken with sorrow, and throw myself into Jesus' arms, for I know how much he loves the prodigal child who returns to him."

One little incident in the life of Thérèse provides us with the perfect Gospel setting for much of what she wants to tell us about repentance. On one occasion she was deeply distressed and returned to the silence of her room. She began to reflect on what Jesus thought of her many faults and failings. "I recalled those words he addressed one day to the adulterous woman," she said, "'Has no one condemned you?' And I answered him with tears in my eyes, 'No one, Lord.'"

A beautiful Gospel scene had flashed across her mind. John, chapter 8, recounts that the scribes and Pharisees brought a woman to Jesus and placed her in full view of everyone: "Master, this woman was caught in the very act of committing adultery," they said. "Moses has ordered us in the Law to condemn women like this to a death by stoning. What have you to say?" Jesus said nothing! He bent down, we are told, and wrote with his finger on the ground. Then he looked up and said: "Let the one who is without sin among you throw the first stone." He bent down again and wrote once more with his finger in the sand. We are not told what he wrote. The hidden sins of the Pharisees? Perhaps. But even if he did, here again we see the mercy of God: their sins were written only to be ruffled by the breeze. Gradually, her accusers slunk away, beginning with the eldest. Jesus was left alone with the woman. Mercy alone with misery! "Woman, where are they? Has no one condemned you?" Jesus asked. "No one," she replied, and you can almost hear the nervous tremor in her voice! "Neither do I condemn you," Jesus said. "Go your way and sin no more." To err is human, to forgive divine.

Thérèse was still quite young when she first discovered the passion of Jesus. She describes the moment for us in her own simple way: "One Sunday, looking at a picture of Our Lord on the cross, I was struck by the blood flowing from one of the divine hands. I felt a great pang of sorrow when thinking this blood was falling to the ground without anyone hastening to gather it up. I was resolved to remain in spirit at the foot of the cross...."

Thérèse then tells the story of "a great criminal" called Pranzini. He was condemned to death for what she calls "some horrible crimes." Everything pointed to the fact that he would die impenitent. But nothing could induce Thérèse to despair. "I offered to God all the infinite merits of Our Lord, the treasures of the Church." She refers to him affectionately as "my sinner." "In the depths of my heart I felt certain that our desires would be granted...I told God I was sure he would pardon the poor, unfortunate Pranzini; that I'd believe this even if he went to his death without any signs of repentance or without having gone to confession. I was absolutely confident in the mercy of Jesus." This is the language of total confidence in God's mercy and the fruits of the passion of Jesus. Then, in her simplicity, Thérèse asked God for a "sign."

The "sign" was given. The day after the execution Thérèse read the newspaper, even against her father's wishes. Her tears betrayed her emotion. These are her own words: "Pranzini had not gone to confession. He had mounted the scaffold and was preparing to place his head in the formidable opening, when suddenly, seized by an inspiration, he turned, took hold of the crucifix the priest was holding out to him, and kissed the sacred wounds three times! Then his soul went to receive the merciful sentence of him who declares that in heaven there will be more joy over one sinner who does penance than over ninety-nine just who have no need of repentance!"

A Fragile Church

Thérèse had many favorite Gospel characters. Peter was one of them—the wild, impetuous Peter. She said she could understand perfectly why he fell: "He was relying upon himself instead of relying on God's grace. Before Peter fell," she continues, "Our Lord said to him, 'and once you are converted, strengthen your brothers.'" Then Thérèse explains what Jesus means: "Convince them of the weakness of human strength through your own experience." In Luke's Gospel, Jesus prayed before he spoke these words to Peter: "Simon, Simon...I have prayed for you that your faith may not fail" (22:31). Jesus did not pray that Peter himself would not fail. He was bound to fail, almost by definition—he was human. Jesus prayed that his faith may not fail. "You are Peter and on this rock...." He is the foundation. Here we have what for many is a new vision of the Church. It is a fragile Church, supported in weakness by the prayer of Jesus. Peter, too, is like everyone else—weak and broken. He needs the mercy of God.

Peter is also a telling example of repentance for Thérèse. He had vehemently protested his loyalty: "Lord, where are you going?" Jesus replied, "Where I am going you cannot follow me now; you will follow me later." Peter said to him, "Why can't I follow you now? I will lay down my life for you." "Will you lay down your life for me?" Jesus asked. And the question is laden with irony for those of us who know the end of the story! He will certainly lay down his life for Jesus, but not in the way Peter thought. "Will you lay down your life for me? I tell you most solemnly, before the cock crows you will deny me three times" (Luke 22:34).

Then the passion trial opens: Are you not also one of this man's disciples?... I am not...and again, I am not...and even again Peter denied it. And at once the cock crowed. Jesus looked at him—a glance of mercy. Peter remembered. He went out and wept bitterly (cf. Luke 22:55–62).

But these events are all background to a later scene which had impressed itself deeply on the mind of Thérèse. Peter stood with the risen Jesus by the lakeside, the same Peter who had denied Jesus three times. Three times he now protests his love: Do you love me?...You know that I love you—once! Do you love me?...You know that I love you—twice! Do you love me? Three times! "Peter was upset that Jesus asked him the third time, 'Do you love me?'" This is a different Peter—chastened, humbled, contrite: "You know all things, O Lord, you know that I love you" (John 21:15–17).

Thérèse had scribbled these words of the chastened Peter on the back of one of her pictures. The scene had touched her. But in the Gospel story, Jesus looks into the future "to show the kind of death by which Peter would give glory to God." Stained-glass windows depicting Peter crucified upside down are quite rare. But Thérèse was familiar with one in the Lisieux cathedral of St. Peter. Jesus reminds Peter once again of his weakness: "When you were young you girded yourself and walked where you liked." Pride ruled his will! Finally, Jesus renews his invitation to Peter, "Follow me" (John 21:19). And so he hobbles along—chastened, wiser, and able—as Thérèse said, "To convince others of the weakness of human strength through his own experience."

Thérèse had a special love for priests and prayed for them in Carmel, but she had no illusions about these anointed vessels of clay. There is great disappointment today at the discovery of clerical failings, and Thérèse knew that disappointment too. She recorded her shock as a young girl at finding that they were, as she said herself, "weak and fragile men who showed in their conduct their extreme need of prayers." To be human is an essential part of what it means to be a priest. The priest is weak and fragile like Jesus because, like Jesus, he is human. To exalt the priest above this shared humanity is to deny the Incarnation: "He can deal gently with the ignorant and the wayward, since he himself is beset with weakness" (Hebrews 5:2).

This is not to minimize in any way the clerical sins and glaring abuses of trust highlighted by the media. These failures have rightly outraged, pained, and angered many, not least the huge majority of priests themselves who are good, committed, and often heroic in their service of the Church. Much support is needed for the scarred victims and their families.

But Thérèse again has a reassuring word. This was how she encouraged a priest-friend worried about his sinful past: "Do you think you frighten me by speaking of your wasted years? I myself thank Jesus who has looked at you with a look of love, as once he looked in the past at the rich young man in the Gospel.... Like me you can sing the mercies of the Lord...love has expelled all fear from my heart. The remembrance of my faults humbles me, draws me never to depend on my strength which is only weakness, but this remembrance speaks to me of mercy and love even more. When we cast our faults with entire confidence like a child into the devouring fire of love, how would these not be consumed—beyond return?"

The Pharisee Within

It is hardly surprising that one Gospel story had a special appeal for Thérèse and she often mentions it. It is the story of the Pharisee and the publican in Luke 18. Luke introduces it with these words: "He told this story to some who trusted in themselves that they were virtuous and despised others." She comments: "Like the publican, I felt I was a great sinner...I found God to be so merciful...my confidence is not lessened." These words may surprise us. As sinners go, Thérèse was not in the top league with Augustine and Mary Magdalene, but she did not miss the point of the parable.

Philosopher Søren Kierkegaard expressed it well when he said: "The greatest Christian heresy is to believe that the opposite of sin is virtue. No, the opposite of sin is grace." The prayer of the publican is a prayer of the helpless, out of the depths of weakness and human failings: "God, be merciful to me, a sinner."

Thérèse had learned the lesson of the story well: "I don't hasten to the first place but to the last;

rather than advance like the Pharisee, I repeat, filled with confidence, the publican's humble prayer. Yes, I feel it; even though I had on my conscience all the sins that can be committed, I would go, my heart broken with sorrow, and throw myself into Jesus' arms."

Thérèse has much to tell us about the Pharisee within the Church. The opposite of sin is not virtue and nobody knew that better than she did. On her deathbed she was told by her sister that she was very patient. She replied, "I haven't even one minute of patience. It's not my patience." We can sense the irritation in her voice when she added: "You always get it wrong." She explained: "To be little is to disown even the virtues that we practice. It's to recognize that God places this treasure in the hands of his little child to be used when necessary. But it remains always God's treasure." Our virtues then are not our virtues. "If I were to say to myself, I have acquired a certain virtue and I am certain I can practice it," she said, "that would be relying upon my own strength." The self-sufficient or so-called "virtuous" still continue to cut themselves off from God's mercy. Thérèse reaffirms a vital Gospel message: we are a fragile Church constantly in need of God's forgiveness.

Obviously, Thérèse did not trust her own virtues. But neither did she despise others less virtuous than she. "I know that without Jesus, I could have fallen as low as St. Mary Magdalene," she said, "but I also know that Jesus has forgiven me more than St. Mary Magdalene since he forgave me in advance by preventing me from falling." This was her way of saying: there but for the grace of God go I!

She was never tempted to throw the first stone. She tried to explain why in a short story. It reads like a parable from the Gospels. Again, it's her favorite image of a little child. We might paraphrase it like this. A doctor has two sons, Thérèse explains, one trips and falls and hurts himself. So the father rushes with all his skill to cure him. The other does not fall, because the father—unobserved!—has removed the stone. Now, Thérèse asks, which of these two sons loved the father more? No doubt, she replies, the first is right to love the father with gratitude in return. The second is unaware of the danger from which he has been saved. So he will not thank the father and will love him less than the first. But, she asks, if he learns about the danger later, will he not love his father more? Well, she says: "I am this child, the object of the foreseeing love of a Father who has not sent his Word to save the just, but sinners. He wants me to love him because he has forgiven me not much but ALL...in order that now I may love him unto folly!"

A Fresh Start

Thérèse provides a whole spirituality based on God's forgiving love. It's her call for repentance or conversion, or a change of mind and heart, a call for a childlike trust in the Father's mercy. But conversion of this kind is not just an isolated moment for Thérèse. Her call is a call for constant repentance over and over again, renewed surrender to God's merciful love. This constant and radical conversion that Thérèse asks for has to be renewed daily. It's a kind of perpetual homecoming. Thérèse knew that she would fall again and again and that she must begin again and again. But she was never discouraged: "If I sometimes fall, through weakness," she prayed, "may your divine gaze purify my soul immediately and burn away all my imperfections, like fire that transforms all things into itself."

One member of her community recalled this story: "I had caused her pain and went to apologize. Looking tenderly at me, she said, 'I have never realized so vividly the love Jesus has for us when we ask him to pardon us for having offended him. If I, his poor little creature, have felt so much love for you when you came back to me, what must happen in the heart of God when we return to him? Most certainly, he will forget all our sins. He will do even more, he will love us far more than before our fault.'"

Thérèse repeats the words of Jesus: "There will be more joy in heaven over one sinner who repents than over ninety-nine righteous persons who have no need of repentance." But she goes even further. She invites us to share that joy. She herself was tempted to despair, but she opened her heart to love and mercy. She knew that in the course of justice none of us would see salvation: "If you want divine justice," she said, "you will get divine justice. The soul gets exactly what it expects from God." We, too, can wallow in despair of forgiveness or we can thrill like Thérèse with confidence and joy: "Joy is not found in the material objects around us," she once said, "but in the inner recesses of the soul. One can possess joy in a prison cell as well as in a palace." It's all in the attitude. She said to one member of her community: "We are not saints who weep for our sins; we rejoice that they serve to glorify the mercy of God." What a source of joy for all eternity! Here she is in line with St. Augustine: "Put your sins beneath your feet," he said, "and they will lift you up to God"; and with Julian of Norwich: "Our forgiven sins will shine like pearls before God and be the cause of our singing the mercies of God for all eternity." John of the Cross wrote: "If there is good or evil in me, love turns them to one sweetness." These words made a deep impression on Thérèse. She repeated them in one of her poems: "Love...knows how to use the good and the bad it finds in me." Yes, even sin!

Thérèse had no fear of judgment; she would be judged by the one she loved: "For those who offer themselves to love, I don't think there will be a judgment at all; on the contrary, God will make haste to reward his own love which he will see in their hearts. We are only consumed by love insofar as we abandon ourselves to love." Thérèse invites us to go to God, not with the misery of our merits, not with the vanity of our virtues, but "with empty hands"; and with her reassuring words echoing in our hearts:

> Living on Love is banishing every fear,
> Every memory of past faults.
> I see no imprint of my sins.
> In a moment love has burned everything...
> Divine Flame, O very sweet Blaze!
> I make my home in your hearth.
> In your fire I gladly sing:
> I live on love...

~

Reflections

The Prodigal's Homecoming

Read Luke 15:11–32

This is perhaps the most consoling story ever told. It's about the painful loss of a son! True, in a sense, he was lost even before he left. He was demanding, without respect, gratitude, or love. Surely, his father was deeply wounded. But still no complaint. The son leaves home for a country far, far away. He squanders his life in loose living and debauchery. He is penniless, helpless, and alone. He wallows with the pigs he tends and shares their food. Shame, distress, and hunger pique his conscience. The scales fall from his eyes. The masks of self-deception drop away. He comes to his senses: "I will arise and go to my Father... I have sinned... I am no longer fit to be called your son...." He had walked freely into misery and darkness. Now he repents and takes the homeward journey into joy and light.

He is like so many of us. He never knew the heart of his father who waits on tiptoe, watching, hoping. At a distance, he sees his son with eyes of compassion, and runs and embraces and kisses him. No excuses needed, no words of repentance, no litany of sins and faults and failings—just a simple cry of sorrow from a repentant son who has strayed from home: "Father, I have sinned against heaven and against you. I no longer deserve to be called your son." All is forgiven. The best robe! New shoes! A new ring on the finger! The prize calf! "My son was dead and is alive. He was lost and is found." This "Welcome Home" was not for the "worthy" son. It was a real celebration—undeserved, unreserved, unbounded joy!

The elder son was dutiful, but loveless. Like so many of us, he was self-righteous, self-sufficient, and he relied on his own observance and was critical of others less "virtuous" than himself. But still no word of condemnation from this loving father. Only words of healing and peace: "All that is mine is yours."

Thérèse understood the story well: "I know how much he loves the prodigal child who returns to him."

Read Luke 18:9–14

Are you running away from something: failures, frustrations, loneliness, guilt, remorse, sinful ways? Are you wandering aimlessly, lost in the maze of life, without a purpose or a meaning? Pause for a moment. The Lord is inviting you to return to him: Come back home again.

Listen to him in the depths of your heart. I am hidden in your loneliness. Search for me there and you will find me—loving, compassionate, tender, forgiving, understanding, consoling, strengthening. Be true to yourself, honest. The truth will set you free. There can be no deception, no masks, no pretense, no affectation, no sham. Pray with the words of the publican: "Lord, be merciful to me a sinner."

Now do what Thérèse asks you to do: banish every fear, every memory of past faults. Your sins have left no trace, she tells you; love has burned everything away in the fire of love.

Persevere in the way of truth. Persevere in prayer.

Prayer

My Joy!

When the blue sky becomes somber
And begins to abandon me,
My joy is to stay in the shadow
To hide and humble myself.

My joy is the Holy Will
Of Jesus, my only love,
So I live without any fear.
I love the night as much as the day.

My joy is to stay little,
So when I fall on the way,
I can get up very quickly,
And Jesus takes me by the hand.
Then I cover him with caresses
And tell Him He's everything for me,
And I'm twice as tender
When He slips away from my faith.

Select Bibliography

St. Thérèse of Lisieux. *Story of A Soul.* A. Clarke Books, 1973.

St. Thérèse of Lisieux. *Collected Letters.* Sheed and Ward, 1975.

Hollings, Michael. *St. Thérèse of Lisieux.* Fount, 1994.

Knox, Ronald. *St. Thérèse of Lisieux.* Fount, 1977.

McCaffrey, Eugene, OCD. *Heart of Love.* Veritas, 1998.

Meester, Conrad. *With Empty Hands.* Burns and Oates, 1987.

JAMES McCAFFREY was born in 1930, in Sligo, Ireland. He entered the Order of Teresian Carmelites in 1948 and obtained a BA at University College, Dublin, in 1954. He subsequently studied at Rome and Jerusalem and returned to Dublin to teach in the Jesuit Institute of Milltown Park, where he was Dean of the Faculty of Theology. He was a Lecturer and Tutor at Ushaw College in Durham and in 1985 became Director of the Carmelite Retreat Centre in Varroville, Sydney. He has lectured widely on the Bible and spirituality in India, Israel, the Philippines, Australia, Africa, New Zealand, Papua New Guinea and the USA. He has also lived for many years in the Holy Land, where he was Superior of the International Carmelite Community in Notre Dame of Jerusalem Centre, and has been editor of *Mount Carmel: A Review of Spirituality* since 1999. Currently based at the Carmelite house at Boars Hill, Oxford, he is Director of the Retreat Centre there and Prior of the community.

His published works include his doctoral thesis: *The House with Many Rooms—The Temple Theme of Jn. 14, 2–3* (*Analecta Biblica* 114) (1988); *Thirsting for God; Prayer—The Heart of the Gospels*; *The Challenge of St. Thérèse*; *St. Thérèse—The Gospels Rediscovered*; and he is co-author, with three other Carmelite biblical specialists, of *A Biblical Prayer Journey in the Holy Land*. He has also contributed articles to numerous publications, including

Spirituality, Religious Life Review and *The Tablet* and, most recently, a chapter to *Ascending the Mountain: The Carmelite Rule Today*. His latest book is *The Carmelite Charism: Exploring the Biblical Roots* and he is currently working on a sequel, *Captive Flames: A Biblical Reading of the Carmelite Saints*.

BOOKS & MEDIA

The Daughters of St. Paul operate book and media centers at the following addresses. Visit, call or write the one nearest you today, or find us on the World Wide Web, www.pauline.org

CALIFORNIA

3908 Sepulveda Blvd, Culver City, CA 90230	310-397-8676
5945 Balboa Avenue, San Diego, CA 92111	858-565-9181
46 Geary Street, San Francisco, CA 94108	415-781-5180

FLORIDA

145 S.W. 107th Avenue, Miami, FL 33174	305-559-6715

HAWAII

1143 Bishop Street, Honolulu, HI 96813	808-521-2731
Neighbor Islands call:	866-521-2731

ILLINOIS

172 North Michigan Avenue, Chicago, IL 60601	312-346-4228

LOUISIANA

4403 Veterans Memorial Blvd, Metairie, LA 70006	504-887-7631

MASSACHUSETTS

885 Providence Hwy, Dedham, MA 02026	781-326-5385

MISSOURI

9804 Watson Road, St. Louis, MO 63126	314-965-3512

NEW JERSEY

561 U.S. Route 1, Wick Plaza, Edison, NJ 08817	732-572-1200

NEW YORK

150 East 52nd Street, New York, NY 10022	212-754-1110

PENNSYLVANIA

9171-A Roosevelt Blvd, Philadelphia, PA 19114	215-676-9494

SOUTH CAROLINA

243 King Street, Charleston, SC 29401	843-577-0175

TENNESSEE

4811 Poplar Avenue, Memphis, TN 38117	901-761-2987

TEXAS

114 Main Plaza, San Antonio, TX 78205	210-224-8101

VIRGINIA

1025 King Street, Alexandria, VA 22314	703-549-3806

CANADA

3022 Dufferin Street, Toronto, ON M6B 3T5	416-781-9131

¡También somos su fuente para libros, videos y música en español!